Publications of the

CENTER FOR EDUCATION IN LATIN AMERICA
Institute of International Studies
Teachers College, Columbia University

LAMBROS COMITAS

GENERAL EDITOR

This series deals with Latin America and the Caribbean—a complex group of countries that defies rigid categorizing. At one level of abstraction, however, it is possible to order the area into three culturally distinctive regions; within each the uniformities of historical development, similarities in the forms of economic exploitation, and equivalencies in size and complexity of indigenous populations have led to structurally similar forms of social organization and articulation. In the Antilles and Circum-Caribbean, the first of these regions, are societies whose institutions bear the imprint of a long colonial heritage and a social legacy from forced connection with Western Europe. Their heterogeneous populations are composed, in most cases, primarily of people with African roots, with important minorities derived from Europe, the Indian subcontinent, China, and the Middle East. A second region, sometimes called Indo-America, includes those countries in the highlands of South and Central America that contain large, culturally viable populations of Amerindians and in which the process of social and cultural integration of native peoples has fundamentally influenced the course and form of nation building. The third region encompasses the societies of the southern, temperate zones of the hemisphere, which demographically and culturally are dominated by the descendants of Europeans. Each book in the series focuses on a particular aspect of one of these countries, or on a particular region, analyses it in detail, and provides the reader the substance that places the educational process, broadly defined, in meaningful context.

WE WISH TO BE LOOKED UPON
A Study of the Aspirations of Youth in a Developing Society
VERA RUBIN AND MARISA ZAVALLONI

GUIDELINES TO PROBLEMS OF EDUCATION IN BRAZIL
A Review and Selected Bibliography
MALVINA R. MCNEIL

BLACK IMAGES
WILFRED G. CARTEY

THE MIDDLE BEAT
A Correspondent's View of Mexico, Guatemala, and El Salvador
PAUL P. KENNEDY

TELLING TONGUES
Language Policy in Mexico, Colony to Nation
SHIRLEY B. HEATH

POLITICS AND THE POWER STRUCTURE
A Rural Community in the Dominican Republic
MALCOLM T. WALKER

STATUS AND POWER IN RURAL JAMAICA
A Study of Educational and Political Change
NANCY FONER

COLONIALISM AND UNDERDEVELOPMENT
Processes of Political Economic Change in British Honduras
NORMAN ASHCRAFT

THE DOMINICAN DIASPORA
From the Dominican Republic to New York City—Villagers in Transition
GLENN HENDRICKS

THE HAITIAN POTENTIAL
Research and Resources of Haiti
VERA RUBIN AND RICHARD P. SCHAEDEL

FRONTIERS IN THE AMERICAS
A Global Perspective
JORGE MAÑACH

Frontiers in the Americas

FRONTIERS IN THE AMERICAS

A Global Perspective

JORGE MAÑACH

A translation by Philip H. Phenix from the Spanish
of the author's *Teoría de la frontera*

teachers college press
TEACHERS COLLEGE, COLUMBIA UNIVERSITY
NEW YORK AND LONDON

Library of Congress Cataloging in Publication Data

Mañach, Jorge, 1898-1961.
  Frontiers in the Americas.

  (Publications of the Center for Education in Latin
America)
  1. Latin America—Relations (general) with the
United States. 2. United States—Relations (general)
with Latin America. 3. Latin America—Civilization.
I. Title. II. Series: Columbia University. Center
for Education in Latin America. Publications.
F1418.M213   301.29'8'073   74-34325
ISBN 0-8077-2481-5
ISBN 0-8077-2480-7 pbk.

Cover design by Lorna Sloan

Introduction

For nearly a quarter of a century, the Cold War distorted international relations and frustrated development in a world badly ravaged by battle and natural calamities. In recent years, however, this peculiar war of the twentieth century has thawed and change in the relationships between nations has become the order of the day. Once the bitterest of enemies, the United States and the Soviet Union are now engaged in diminishing tensions and forging closer ties. China and the United States grope for understanding and eventual rapprochement. Other major political anomalies are in the process of being resolved. The rupture of relations between Cuba and the United States, for example, may well be mended in the very near future. For the Western Hemisphere, this latter case is of particular significance.

It may appear paradoxical that the yet to be achieved opening of the frontier between two countries separated physically by only a few miles of tranquil sea has been so long delayed and has been accompanied by such enmity. With others, I would argue that the prolongation of this unnecessary breach is not just a petulant reaction by the United States to political heresy, or a refusal to compromise political principles by the Cuban revolutionary leadership, but rather a more fundamental consequence of the effects of the long subordination of Latin America to the United States. One curious but nonetheless pernicious corollary of this unequal relationship has been a marked lack of understanding between the two spheres, epitomized by the dominant power's virtual ignorance of the values and sensibilities central to Latin American thought and action. The blunt truth is that the United States, despite contiguity and self-interest, knows relatively less about its non-Anglo-Saxon neighbors south of the Rio Grande than it does about many of the populations of other major world regions. On the other side of the coin, Latin Americans tend to hold often misleading, stereotypic views about the Colossus of the North.

It is the very essence of this involuted and critical problem that is addressed in this posthumous work by Jorge Mañach, a son of Cuba, Antillean patriot, and above all, a man of intellect and vision. More than thirteen years after his death, at a time of diplomatic breakthroughs and new hope, Mañach's insightful analysis of the meaning of the frontier retains a quality and freshness that illuminates and clarifies a fundamental aspect of the American condition.

I am more than pleased to welcome this unique and important contribution to the series, and to express my gratitude to Professor Philip Phenix, eminent philosopher and scholar of Latin American values who, appreciating the worth of Jorge Mañach's thought, undertook the demanding task of translating these pages into English and carried the project through to its fruition.

LAMBROS COMITAS

Translator's

Preface

F ew questions strike so close to the heart of the contemporary
world's life as that of the frontiers that separate peoples,
nations, and cultures. In an age of increasing interdependence, the
isolation of segments of the human family is no longer possible.
Moreover, as the forms of mutuality become increasingly vital to the
survival and development of each part, the nature of the interfaces
between peoples becomes a matter of fundamental concern.

For Americans, perhaps no question of frontiers is more important than that concerning the relations between North America and
Latin America. As the United States has increased in power over the
years to the point of becoming the richest and strongest nation on
earth, the peoples of Latin America have all too often been relegated
to a position of secondary importance in the thought and practice of
North Americans. Such a situation violates not only basic canons of
justice and equity, but also bodes ill for the peace, prosperity, and
human development of all American nations, including the United
States itself. The future well-being of the entire Western Hemisphere
and of each of its parts depends on the growth of forms of mutual
understanding and cooperation between the peoples with Latin traditions and those with predominantly Anglo-Saxon traditions.

Fortunately for the feasibility of this enterprise in mutuality, the
sort of ignorance and neglect that have so commonly characterized
the North American attitude toward Latin America is not characteristic of Latin Americans. The latter, precisely because they have had
to adjust and adapt to the presence of the great power to the north,
have generally been keenly aware of the nature of their relationship
to that power, and sensitive interpreters within the Latin American
cultural tradition have concerned themselves with these relations.

One of the dominant themes in Latin American writing over the
years has been the nature of Latin American culture in comparison
to and in contrast with that of the United States. Probably no work

in the Spanish-speaking world has been so influential in this regard as the celebrated essay by the Uruguayan writer José Enrique Rodó entitled *Ariel*, written just following the Spanish-American War. In this essay the author compared the two great cultures of the hemisphere, portraying the United States, under the figure of Caliban, as concerned with efficiency and utility, and Latin America, under the figure of Ariel, as dedicated primarily to aesthetic and spiritual values.

A little more than half a century later another distinguished man of letters, Jorge Mañach, a Cuban, prepared a series of lectures in which he extended, updated, and gave theoretical foundations to the kind of concerns that were central to Rodó and that have occupied an important place in the consciousness of all the leading thinkers of Latin America. The present book comprises these lectures, which were to have been delivered at the University of Puerto Rico. The fulfillment of this task was unfortunately frustrated by the author's death on June 26, 1961. Happily, through the dedicated efforts of his friend and colleague, Concha Meléndez, a noted Puerto Rican scholar and professor of Hispanic studies at the University of Puerto Rico, the lectures were edited and published in 1969 by the press of the university, with an introduction by Professor Meléndez, which appears here as an appendix.

These lectures are now offered to the English-speaking public in the present translation, published by Teachers College Press in cooperation with the Center for Education in Latin America of Teachers College, Columbia University. In this effort the encouragement and cooperation of the center's director, Professor Lambros Comitas, well-known anthropologist with special interest and competence in the Caribbean area and Latin America generally, have been decisive and are hereby gratefully acknowledged. The translator also wishes to thank Margot B. Mañach, widow of Jorge Mañach, for her interest in this translation and for granting permission to publish it.

Jorge Mañach was singularly fitted for the task of writing a fundamental work on the frontiers of America. He was born in Cuba in 1898, at the close of the Spanish-American War, and at the beginning of the epoch during which relations between the two great cultures of the Americas have become most decisive for the peace and prosperity of the hemisphere and the world. He was educated in Cuba, the United States, Spain, and France, and held degrees from both Harvard University and the University of Havana. He taught Hispanic literature at Columbia University in New York from 1935 to 1939 and was for many years professor of philosophy at the University of Havana.

Accordingly, Mañach had direct personal understanding of life on both sides of the frontier between the Latin American and North American cultures. He was a tireless exponent of Hispanic culture for North Americans and a devoted intellectual leader among his compatriots in Latin America, to whom he was able to render unusual service as a knowledgeable critic and interpreter of North American life as well as an articulator of Latin American traditions and aspirations.

Mañach was a prolific writer. Interestingly, his literary efforts began in English as co-editor of a little high school magazine in Cambridge, Massachusetts, during the year 1916. He published his first book in 1924 in Cuba and from then on the tide of his literary production swelled so that ultimately his bibliography included more than eight-thousand items. He was most productive in the field of journalism, but he published in many fields, including drama—he wrote an award-winning play. He was best known for his essays, particularly in the area of aesthetic criticism. Probably his most widely read work is his moving biography of the great Cuban patriot José Martí, (1853-1895), which was translated into English under the title *Martí, Apostle of Freedom.* At the time of his death, Mañach was far along with two major works: *History of Philosophy,* a product of his many years of research and teaching in that field, and a book entitled *The Formation of the Cuban Conscience,* a comprehensive study of the life and thought of José Martí.

It is natural that Jorge Mañach should have devoted so much of his thought and writing to the great Martí, for there were notable similarities between the two men. Both were extraordinarily gifted as writers and speakers on a wide range of topics. Both were concerned with the dissemination of knowledge for the creation of an informed public consciousness. In 1932 Mañach organized a university of the air in Havana, as one may surmise Martí would have done had modern instruments of communication been available in his day. Thus he initiated a kind of radio and television broadcasting that had great and salutary influence on the public life of Cuba from that time forward.

Like Martí, Mañach was deeply devoted to his native land. In 1940 he was elected senator from Cuba's Oriente Province, as he had earlier been a delegate from his native Las Villas Province to the constituent convention that drafted the constitution of 1940. But, like Martí, Mañach was no ordinary politician primarily bent on gaining and holding power. He entered political life solely to serve his country and help her realize her highest ideals, of which he was one of the leading spokesmen.

In reading Mañach, as in reading Martí, one is struck with the author's concern for truth rather than for partisan persuasiveness. Political life in Cuba during Mañach's lifetime was far from tranquil. He suffered exile in the 1930s, finding a refuge and useful employment for his talents in academic work at Columbia University. He was again in exile during the last year of his life. He had welcomed the new era that seemed to be dawning with the revolution led by Fidel Castro, but soon discovered that illiberal forces were at work under the new regime, which shattered his hopes for a truly democratic Cuba. Despite these experiences of disillusion and the defeat of his fondest hopes and expectations for his beloved country, Mañach in his writings did not engage in partisan polemic and never lost the irenic spirit of one who seeks only to know the truth and to serve the interests of freedom and justice.

It is this irenic quality that gives the lectures that form this book a high degree of permanent relevance and validity. Mañach, like Ortega y Gasset, the eminent Spanish philosopher and man of letters who was also a teacher of his people, did not reason in abstractions only, but with profound awareness of historical circumstances and concrete cultural realities. For this reason, Mañach's treatment of the theory of the frontier in this book is clearly set within the particular context of our time and makes specific reference to particular events and conditions of the contemporary era. Nevertheless, the treatment is so fundamental in its conceptual terms and analytic method that its message far transcends the particularities of its immediate present. Accordingly, although the reader in a few places in the text will recognize the atmosphere of the Kennedy era, the Alliance for Progress, Operation Bootstrap, and the early Castro years, these specifics in no way obtrude on the argument nor condition it in such a way as to render the development of the thesis any less valid for the current scene than for the 1960s.

It is the translator's hope that Mañach's wise reflections in these lectures may be of service in stimulating the kind of creative dialogue between Latin America and North America that Mañach so fervently longed for and that will do so much to enrich the life of all America.

PHILIP H. PHENIX
Arthur I. Gates Professor of
Philosophy and Education

Teachers College
Columbia University

Contents

I

Concerning the

Frontier in General

You already know how much we Cubans are inclined, in the most diverse circumstances, to make use of the thought and words of our José Martí. That is part of a fervent patriotic devotion, which, like all cults, does not escape a certain ritualism and even pious affectation. But there is a sentence from our noble countryman that I can apply in all sincerity to the present occasion: "In the generosity of a eulogy is disclosed, not the merit of the one eulogized, but the magnanimous heart of one who gives more praise than is due."

In the words with which Rector Benítez bid me welcome to this university, he only revealed his unbounded generosity, condensing in a cordial compact summary all the hospitality and the honor of which he had already made me the object, in the name of the University of Puerto Rico, in giving me access to this institution of learning.

I would not want it to appear that I respond to so great a tribute merely with gestures of gratitude. Rather I would feel I was leaving unpaid the homage due if I did not say that—not just for an unassuming professor like myself, but for the most eminent in any part of the academic world—it is an honor to come to teach in these classrooms. Perhaps you yourselves, because of the demands of your task, do not clearly realize to what degree the University of Puerto Rico so brilliantly displays Latin American culture. The attraction that its prestige and its intellectual drive exercise—aided by all the blessings of this island and by the hospitality of its people—is shown by the many outstanding figures in the intellectual and aesthetic domain, including some of the most glorious of our tongue, who have passed through and remained, as it were, captivated and captured here.

1

Among those no longer living, I cannot fail to recall Gabriela Mistral, Juan Ramón Jiménez, and Pedro Salinas. I was united to them by a friendship as deep as my admiration. It will always seem that their beloved shadows are wandering beneath the bowers and arches of your university campus. Thanks to those glorious presences, those absent glorious ones, a fragrant emanation of poetry descends, like a benediction, from the summit of your heraldic tower.

As a veteran of the university world, a bit hardened by the vicissitudes of academic life, I bear witness that in other universities in Spain and both Americas—including, of course, the University of Havana from which I come—this university is regarded with lively fellow-feeling and profound respect. And all of its sister institutions are affected by the busy hum of the beehive of students and professors who safeguard these achievements. The sense both of the present and of the future that they impart to their tasks, the calm disquietude—so different from certain extravagant and vociferous agitations I well know—and the concern that routines will not lull to sleep their sense of responsibility in higher education, all work to confront the great demands of the society and the individual that have made themselves so pressing in our time.

In spite of a certain burden of patriotic melancholy, I feel happy to be among you, gentlemen, and most honored to be able to share in those tasks. May the youthful countenance of Minerva continue always to watch over this university, still so young and yet so illustrious!

The Theme and Its Scope

I do not know if I shall hit the mark in thinking that this university conceives her specific mission—apart from the basic one of every institution of this type—as one of supporting, with the most concentrated energy at her disposal, the joining of the two great cultures of America in their zone of maximum interaction. At least that is the impression I have received from reading certain admirable speeches of Rector Benítez and other official documents. I would not be able to add anything substantive to them within their purely academic context. But in their rich succinctness they raise more general problems. In any case, that impression suggested to me the theme of the addresses I am beginning today: the frontier, particularly our cultural frontier with the United States, viewed not only on its own terms, but also insofar as it represents or symbolizes the actual and possible relations between the two Americas.

I am well aware that even defined this broadly the theme is not new, especially in Puerto Rico. For obvious reasons, you have become keenly conscious of the situation to which it refers, since not only are you located on the boundary line between the two great divisions of the hemisphere, but also because a special political connection links you with the United States. But it is well to remember that at least geographically and culturally the frontier situation is not peculiar to you. It is shared by all of the Latin American countries that find themselves in a contiguous relation to the United States, including my own island. Thus this really quite peaceful incursion of mine into the frontier, that is into the area of problems it poses, is in no sense an intrusion; it may be that if I can shed some new light on this theme it will be that which with luck will come from taking a more comprehensive perspective on the subject.

Perhaps then we shall be able to see that the question goes beyond the frontier itself and that in some way it concerns the destiny of all of our America, since frontiers are usually like extremities whose nerve fibers extend to the whole body that they bound and to the whole human mass for which they serve as means of communication and contact. Surely in this respect the theme of the American frontier has now taken on special relevance. As a result of the recent election of Mr. Kennedy to national leadership, there is much talk in the United States of a new orientation in the relations of that country with our America, an "alliance for progress," which in turn seems to be part of a policy called the New Frontier. Will it not behoove us Latin Americans also to say something about this?

Finally, the question suggests even broader problems. The most sanguine utopianists of all time dream of a world without frontiers; others dream of a classless society. Quite apart from such idealizations, we all know that today the world finds itself divided by a vast ideological frontier over which hovers, in the turbulence and tensions of the Cold War, the greatest threats and dangers the world has ever confronted, because they involve the destiny of all humanity.

Although it is not my purpose to touch more than incidentally on these questions of universal scope—we already have enough to do trying to clarify what the frontier means for the peoples of our hemisphere and for Latin Americans in particular—the theme has continued to expand before my eyes as I have approached it. Above all, it became clear to me that it was not possible to approach the cultural frontier without first going through the political and economic ones. I beg your indulgence for thus availing myself overmuch of the attention with which you honor me. At least this will have the advantage of permitting us to see the foundations upon which the problem of the cultural frontier rests, which is what arouses our main interest on the present occasion.

Today, then, we shall set forth certain considerations about frontiers in general. In the next lecture, we shall be concerned with political and economic frontiers. The third and fourth will give us an opportunity to describe and compare the two great American cultures that face one another on the cultural frontier. The final one will refer to the sort of relations that ought to exist, and do now exist in Puerto Rico to an appreciable degree, although not without giving rise to some very delicate problems. I sincerely thank you for your perseverance in accompanying me on this extended inquiry, which I hope will not leave us all exhausted.

What Is a Frontier?

Let us begin with some obvious and elementary notions. Possibly from them may flow others not so simple.

If we adhere to the authority of the geographers, the ones who professionally understand these things, frontier means simply the limits or confines of a territory that is invested with a certain independence. The line, demarcation, or boundary that separates two provinces of the same country are not, then, frontiers. In contrast, coasts are, as we recall from our first school readers, and so frontiers are divided into terrestrial and maritime.

Let us agree, however, that the terrestrial frontiers are the most characteristic, since only they *confront*—and from that the word is derived*—two zones of superior authority, two states. On maps, these divisions are represented graphically, sometimes by a rectilinear neatness that betrays the conventional origin of the frontier, at other times by little serpents that stand for rivers and small centipedes that symbolize chains of mountains. But we know that if geography is a basic condition for the frontier, it nevertheless does not constitute its essence. Its more profound reality reveals itself to us in traveling, when we see that at a certain point in our journey one authority disappears and another emerges, which generally imposes on us rather annoying customs and security procedures. Even in the cases where by chance this does not happen, we always have the sensation, in crossing a frontier, of having entered a different environment, where the people and even the things display a certain intimacy in relation to one another in the same degree that they become strange in relation to us, the travelers.

We notice, then, that the frontier—beyond being a physical or merely political reality—is one of a psychological, social, and cultural order. The dividing line between states of very similar traditions and

---

*In Spanish the parallel between *frontera* and *enfrentar* to which Mañach alludes is similar to that between 'frontier' and 'confront' in English.—*Tr.*

culture, like Canada and the United States, or like France and Belgium, appears to us as barely a frontier. The same holds for the lines that separate our Latin American republics on the continent, to such an extent that the disputes in which they occasionally embroil themselves for the sake of those boundaries strike us as painfully childish. By contrast, the political link that exists between Puerto Rico and the United States does not and will not prevent your island from being a land with a true frontier as long as it fosters a tradition, a calling, and a culture different from those of North America.

The frontier situation, then, implies relations of physical contiguity and of opposition, or at least of differences, between two complexes of interests. As regards proximity, it is important to note that it need not be one of absolute immediacy. The body of water that separates the Antilles from the United States serves as a frontier no less than the Río Grande, across which Mexicans and North Americans look at one another's faces, or sometimes only their backs. One might even ask if that strip of sea is not the real frontier, and our islands only borderlands. Presently we shall see that in this case, which is so important to us, the sea acts as an element both of contiguity and of separation, as a filter of influences and as a shock absorber.

Concerning the relations of opposition that the most authentic frontiers represent, the disparate interests may be more or less varied and deep. Thus, it is clear that the word "frontier" far transcends just the political meaning.

The Hierarchy of Frontiers

So, there is a variety of frontiers. We speak of the Pyrenees as the frontier between Spain and France, yet in the history of the peninsula one also reads much about the frontier facing the Moors, and in United States history about the western frontier. Prior to the more or less stabilized political frontiers, there were the mobile frontiers of wars and conquests. Even within such situations of fluidity, auxiliary frontiers of less note but not always less importance are sometimes formed. Thus, it could be said that within the broad context of the initial North American expansion, for example, the frontier of the colonists against the Indians was preceded by that of the fur traders, that of the missionaries, and even that of the invasion of certain diseases, which apparently were the first gift from the Old World to America, the first form of imperialism imposed upon her. We also speak of economic, ethnological, and religious frontiers— like those of the Reformation struggle in Renaissance Europe, and we speak of cultural frontiers in general. Finally, it is common

knowledge that today there are ideological frontiers of unprece-
dented abruptness, across which face one another—even within the
same city, as happens in Berlin—not merely types of social and political regimes, but radically opposed philosophic conceptions of the
world.

One may say that these other uses of the word "frontier" presuppose a metaphorical extension. That is true. But the metaphors
would not be valid, that is intelligible, unless they rested upon af-
finities and resemblances. Common to all of those uses of the word
frontier is the dual relation of contiguity and contrariety. Within that
general class, frontiers are distinguished or defined by the nature of
the interests or purposes that face one another, or which we particularly want to emphasize.

These range from the rude covetousness of primitive conquest,
on through the most tortuous calculations of politics and economics
and the historic tensions between cultures, to the endeavor, so evident today in the world, to impose certain systems of ideas—and to
defend oneself from them. On a higher level, the more ethereal the
frontier and the more subtle the forces that struggle there, the more
involved are the problems presented. However, there are physical
frontiers in which diverse interests meet—political, economic, ethnic,
and cultural—embracing the broadest and the narrowest, like the
spheres in certain Chinese toys that carry inside a whole brood of
lesser spheres. Those complex frontiers are, of course, the most sensitive and problematic, though not necessarily the ones that generate
the most activity in the world. Ours with the United States is one of
them.

But presently we shall come to that. Now we have to look a bit
more deeply into the essence of every frontier, not as a game of abstraction, but because it proves useful for all we have to say later.

Frontier and Power

Contiguity and opposition are not merely manifestations of the
frontier, or more precisely, of the forces that face one another at the
frontier. As we have just seen, these forces may be military, political,
economic, or simply spiritual: the pressures and the resistances of
different peoples with conflicting beliefs, cultures, or ideologies. Obviously the essence of all force, that which causes it to be force, is its
power. We commonly think of this only as human force; nevertheless,
we do speak of a powerful machine, of the firepower of an army, of
electric power, and of horsepower.

Now then, in purely human terms, if you will, what is power? I
do not know if anybody has ever formulated a philosophy of power

in a special and exclusive form, that is, not as part of some philosophical system. I refer not to a philosophy of the *exercise* of power, which is an old theme from Aristotle to Raymond Aron, with Machiavelli in between, but a philosophy of *power itself*, of the very essence of power. There is a philosophy of authority, for example, the one in the book of that title by Giuseppa Rienzi—a book that seemed admirable to me when I read it a few years ago, among other things because of the keen realism with which certain soft political idealisms are punctured and deflated in its pages. But let us agree that authority is not the same as power. In order to demonstrate that, allow me to mention the Mexican story of the bum who is in a public place relieving himself. A policeman catches him at it and warns him that it can't be done. "No?" replies the offender, "Then how come I'm doing it?"

What this suggests in its simple way is that power is primarily and essentially a *capacity* that depends only on the will of those possessing to it to produce an effect. It is therefore prior to authority. Authority emanates from power, and not vice versa. A subordinate official may have authority, but he receives it from one who has more authority and ultimately from one who has power. Although legal and administrative parlance speaks of the delegation of powers, strictly speaking power as such is never delegated. What is delegated is authority or dominion, the capacity to act in the name of the power. Were it not to take us too far afield, it could be shown that that proposition contains the germ of a whole philosophy of democracy. The latter is a regime in which authority emanates from the power of the people. By contrast, authoritarian regimes are those that make power derive from authority, from pure dominion.

But we are more interested for the moment in emphasizing that power is something that can be exercised or not, as one wishes. There is an edifying adage to the effect that "to will is to be able." But that equation involves a miniature moral philosophy rather than an ontology of power itself. The maxim is only true in the sense that wanting to, the will, is what sets in motion the power, that which actualizes the desire. There is, then, a potential power and an actual or acting power.

Perhaps I will be asked what all of this has to do with the frontier. A great deal, I believe. In order to suggest what, let us again make use of concrete examples. Let us take those that are as close at hand as possible. Few will deny that Latin America would like to be as rich, as strong, and as influential in worldly things as the United States. It *would like to;* but it *cannot;* at least now, it cannot. Let us invert the example. The United States, at a certain stage in its history, carried the frontier with Latin America to the point where it wished to extend the power it possessed. Later, at another stage of its development, it *was able* to continue extending that frontier, but it *did not want to.* We are not concerned at the moment with discussing whether these assertions are true or not; it is sufficient that you admit them as likely. Surely they are not farfetched. There are many people who ask themselves—and we will have to put the question to ourselves in the course of these lectures—if Latin America might have been able to do more than it did in facing up to the United States, and why the United States, for its part, halted its expansive power at the Río Grande and at the arc of the Antilles. Finally, there are many who ask themselves what would have happened in our America, what would happen even now if, instead of the United States, Russia, for example, were our neighbor and the power dominating the hemisphere.

But the conclusion at which I now want to arrive is this: What is essential at the frontier, at any frontier, are the forces that confront and oppose one another, and that the power of those forces does not necessarily have to be accompanied by a will that impels them. On the economic frontier, the forces in their blind mechanism are generally able to function with maximum efficacy by themselves. On ethnic, religious, and cultural frontiers, oppositions of different races, beliefs, and cultures suffice to create frontiers without the intervention of any will. On the "ideological" frontier the will does intervene in order to turn beliefs into more or less dogmatic ruling impulses. But it is above all on the political frontier—which includes the military, and frontiers resulting from conquest—where the will is, by definition, indispensable. The political frontier is *the place to which the will carries the power at its disposal.* It is the *actualized* will.

Perspectives on the Frontier

I would like to offer one further preliminary consideration, or rather substantiate and emphasize it, since I dropped a hint of it in my initial comments. Your acceptance of it will depend on your not thinking that I have broadened the scope of our theme too much. It has to do with the extension or range of the phenomenon we are discussing.

Geographically, the frontier is first of all a *situs,* a place, a locus of confluence and contact of distinct areas. Like every situation, it implies a system of relations. These are, in the first place, those that exist between the two contiguous zones that the frontier separates; but also those that are established between the frontier and the whole social mass that it outlines, which may be only a town, or a nation, or—as in the case of the American frontier on the side facing us—a whole constellation of nations. On the frontier, then, two types of problems present themselves: those that are concerned exclusively with the frontier, and others that embrace as well the much greater domain of which the frontier is a sort of essence and distillation, or at least a kind of symbol.

In some contemporary psychology with an existential orientation, frequent use is made of the concept of situation and particularly of so-called limit situations, which are those that involve the root meaning of human existence, those in which the whole being of the person is at stake. Without pretending to establish any equivalence between things as different as the spiritual and the geographical, we could say metaphorically that the physical frontier, with its political, economic, and cultural appurtenances, is in its own way a limit situation, since it highlights the circumstances, interests, and problems common to it and the hinterland; that is to say, to the entire historical *persona* for which it serves as face or countenance. It follows that the theme of the inter-American frontier not only permits us, but even obliges us, to deal with the entire system of relations between the United States and Latin America.

After these abstractions, which I hope have not proven as tedious to you as they have seemed useful to me, we can move on toward more concrete territory. But not without a few more general observations.

Genesis and End

One such general consideration is the question of why frontiers have to exist at all. The genesis of frontiers would be an interesting theme in itself, since it can be supposed that their source is not limited just to the remote past, but transcends the actual beginning and end of such dividing lines. Unfortunately, the question inevitably falls into the area of pure speculation, tempting us to adventure too far into the mysteries of the Creation itself, or at least of the primordial human condition, on both of which matters we do not yet have any scientific certainty. The theologians will have to be the ones to decide whether unity or variety was in the original divine plan, just as they have determined that ambition was not born with Adam but was payment for original sin. We might instead, as I prefer, adopt the wonderful insight of José Hernández's gaucho, the memorable Martín Fierro:

> One is the sun, one is the world,   The being of all beings
> only and one is the moon;   Unity alone made it;
> thus is known that God   all else man made
> created no quantity at all.   after he learned to count.

What is certain is that within history people appeared already endowed with different aptitudes for satisfying their common wants —for example, some were more adept than others in attacking and defending themselves. Having at their disposal, as they did, so ample a world in which to live at ease, they promptly began to quarrel over it on the grounds of climate, food supply, security, or even of pure exclusiveness or adventurous impulse. Covetousness of what belongs to another and jealousy for one's own seem to have been the mainsprings of action in history. We seem to be so made that only through special gifts of kindness in certain individual natures or thanks to the refinements of culture do we come to treat our neighbor in a neighborly way. Who does not know how frequent, especially in old societies, are the traditional rivalries between inhabitants of the same area? When in a popular celebration, for example, the young men of one village get too close to those of the next village, the encounter commonly ends up in a fight. Sex also has a lot to do with it. One of the first violations of the frontier must have been the famous abduction of the Sabine women. Mythology, which is not always wholly a matter of fantasy, assures us that Europe itself was born of an abduction. God alone knows if she is to come to her death in the same way.

Was the economic factor even more decisive? Was the multiplication of frontiers due to the fact that, as Martín Fierro says, man "learned to count"? In this matter, how much credence are we to give to Marxism?

Much has been written about Spain's Golden Age when, according to Cervantes, mortals did not distinguish between thine and mine. If such a brilliant era really existed, it must have occurred, paradoxically, in the darkest recesses of prehistory, since no appreciable signs of it have remained. As regards the social order, the most valid conjectures of the anthropologists, as I understand them, refer to the Iron Age. It appears that already at that time collective appropriation existed, and that only much later private appropriation followed. With the former, frontiers must have arisen, and with the latter, just as clearly, social classes.

In any case, one cannot resist the temptation to link both types of "barriers" historically, as they doubtless associate themselves psychologically and perhaps sociologically. Indeed, even today it can happen that such barriers are created and more energetically sustained in countries where land is of high value and that, inversely, they are not clearly marked, at least politically, in countries where there is generally less concern over wealth. We can make this much of a concession to the Marxist position: The economic factor is one element, though it is by no means always the sole determinant. Let us also grant that it is in the capitalist countries that the idea of "a world without frontiers" tends to be regarded as the ideal. Up to now the most they have attempted, as in Europe during *la belle époque,* is travel without passports, and that was generally ephemeral. As soon as even the threat of war arose, the frontiers became prominent again, like distended veins in the people's countenance.

Nevertheless, such attempts at internationalization continue to be significant. It seems that the world's conscience is pricked by its own particularisms. None will deny that down through history mankind has increasingly felt called toward universalism. If not from the Golden Age, the idea did appear in the twilight of Greco-Roman culture, when the Stoics and even the Epicureans boasted of being citizens of the world. Through medieval ecumenism this noble yearning was transmitted to the Renaissance, giving its noblest radiance to the very conception of Humanism, Natural Right, and the Right of Peoples. Projected across the broad seas, the dream that had emerged from the Renaissance utopias enveloped virginal America with the halo of a land called to the realization of human fraternity, liberty, and justice. In that image the finest of the "American intelligence" has been nourished—recalling Alfonso Reyes's phrase and concept.

We do not know if it will ultimately be man's lot to fulfill the glorious dream of the Golden Age, when there will be no private property, nor classes, nor frontiers. I have my doubts. But we have already come a long way in having dreamed of it. And may we continue to dream of it, provided it does not give us nightmares like this one of the Cold War, in which that vision is so confusedly invoked. What I want to underscore is that, in spite of the fierce proclivities that Hobbes and other pessimists attribute to the human condition, in the long course of time—particularly modern times—mankind has been opening up avenues of cooperation that are no less persistent for being insecure and difficult. At times it almost appears that today we may already be witnessing, even in that paradoxical affair of the Cold War, the final battle in search of the "one world" of which the lamented Wendell Willkie spoke, and that even those latest faustian accomplishments in nuclear science and the conquest of astral space may be a kind of prelude to a vast harmony into which the interests and the ideals of the whole world are called finally to integrate themselves.

The Frontier in History

If we take into account the variety of perspectives on the frontier of which I spoke earlier, it would be no exaggeration to affirm that the entire history of the world could be explained in terms of different types of frontiers. This holds true on not only the most ostensible plane of conquests and conflicts, but also on that of what may be termed the inward formation of peoples. Though frontiers have their risks and burdens, there are times when they are not lacking in great and beneficent possibilities. What may be objectionable in them from the point of view of human solidarity is somewhat compensated for by their having also served in many cases to stimulate a people toward greater efforts in defining and developing their collective personality.

Particularly in the stages of creating a nation, the social mass to which the frontier is due tends to impregnate itself with the spirit that develops there and sustain itself with the frontier's energies. A celebrated example was ancient Greece, which we must so often invoke for her unfailingly excellent instruction. This great enigma was greatly favored by her privileged location at the convergence of the four great zones of the world that surrounded her. But we know that the place where the great Hellenic culture germinated was in the colonies of Asia Minor, particularly Ionia where Troy had been. Beyond that vigorous border, where the East looks out over the Mediterranean, was the Persian Empire. Its power, which was not merely military, represented for Greece what Toynbee calls a challenge. On that frontier the Greeks lived more tensely, more alertly, eager to use every kind of resource in the face of the Asiatic threat. From that state of mind was born an intense spiritual activity, the determined application of intelligence to speculation and to practical inquiries, and the heroic sense of life. There tragic and lyric poetry, art, science, and philosophy budded and prospered. The so-called "miracle of Greece" began on the frontier.

In the military and political realm, Roman history affords a scarcely less apt example. The great city, like the Italian country districts, provided consuls and patricians; but the schools of generals and the breeding grounds of caesars were on the frontiers. On them originated all of the roads that went to Rome. The latter maintained itself proudly and with true majesty as long as those peripheral muscles of the body politic kept their tone and elasticity. Contrary to what is commonly thought, the relaxation of the frontiers was what contributed most decisively to the demoralization of the glorious city, and not the reverse. On the other hand, those very borders of the empire served ultimately as the viaducts or streams of vitality and culture that came to transform the substance of the classical world, illustrating the two-fold potential, positive and negative, that frontiers possess.

In the Spain of the Reconquest, the no-man's land between Christians and Moors was an area both of struggle and of frequently creative association. In it the harsh thrust of El Cid and the polished courtliness of the caliphates, whose culture extended into the Christian world from Córdoba and Toledo, confronted and reciprocally modified each other. The eminent Gregorio Marañón even came to see Toledo as the living witness of the frontier between the whole Orient and Europe. From that contact between the Christian and the Islamic was born a feeling of solidarity underlying the warlike antagonism, a chivalrous sense of the fight itself and of life in general, which as we know flowered with singular beauty in the romances and frontier stories. From all of that Castile was being formed, and Castile made the nation.

Let us make a great leap in time and space. In North America the frontier also contributed decisively to the nation's formation. That thesis was first formulated in 1893 by Frederick Jackson Turner, then professor at the University of Wisconsin, in a monograph entitled *The Significance of the Frontier in American History*. The idea caught on. Not many years later George Santayana adopted it, adding the Puritan tradition as another of the ingredients of the national heritage. In the face of the expansive, daring, pugnacious spirit of individual and autonomous effort that the frontier created, Puritanism represented a certain counterweight of moral discipline, destined in time to transcend its purely religious bounds. I believe that thesis is valid, and later I am going to depend on it heavily.

Will it be considered an exaggeration if I say that in our Latin America the influence of the frontier has also been very powerful or that our countries became vigorous in the degree to which they received that influence? The conquest produced as many frontiers as there were conquerors. Each one first hatched its own colonial unity and later its respective independence and national character. In Chile, the struggle against the Araucanos, which lasted from the time of Ercilla's epic poem until well into the nineteenth century, contributed to the strong sense of nationality and the keynote of militancy that characterizes Chileans. Brazil nurtured its first impulses toward independence in the expansion of the frontier by the *bandeirantes*. It is largely due to the United States imperialist dismemberment of Mexico that for her people her northern frontier continues to feel like the living flesh of an amputated limb and so they are inspired by the most intense nationalism on our part of the continent. It is hardly necessary to recall how much Argentina owes to the struggles and the shiftings of her frontier, for social and political as well as spiritual stimulus. The story of these battles is the subject of increasingly exalted literary expression, beginning with Sarmiento's *Facundo*—the rural district bosses in our America were almost always a characteristic species of the frontier—to Güiraldes's *Don Segundo Sombra*, with the immortal gaucho epic *Martín Fierro* in between.

Emblem of conquest, herald of independence, school of rebels in civil strife, for almost all of our countries on the continent the frontier served as the grinding edge on which the nation's temperament was whetted, and when civilization tamed its fierceness, it became the theme of elegies on the collective spirit and a source of noble inspiration.

The General Function of the Frontier

Even the purely geographical frontier, without larger historical associations or political implications, everywhere has a function that can be a source of ennoblement, although also of debasement. Once the regressive energy with which a distinctive character is imparted to the social mass outlined by the frontier is exhausted, the external boundary generally constitutes, so to speak, an *abrasive surface* that keeps the collective consciousness on the alert. It is common knowledge that peoples without polemical frontiers tend to abandon themselves to a more or less vegetative inertia. They lose personality, aggressiveness, and competitive vigor. In Switzerland, which is certainly a model if there is any, a culture was created that was more industrious than creative and more peaceful than heroic. On the other hand, people such as the Paraguayans in our America, caught between the frontiers of ambitious neighbors, exhibit a long tradition of intense and fierce nationalism, which tends to have a corresponding debasement: a sort of spiritual withdrawal and rugged provincialism that is sometimes barbarous and never very propitious for ease of communication with those outside, or for the most subtle refinements of patriotic feeling.

The defining influence that frontiers exert on peoples in their formative periods is extinguished as they reach maturity. Then the frontier ceases to be a dynamic and pivotal factor and changes into something static and peripheral. If the struggle that gave rise to the dividing line is maintained in a latent state with actual or potential matching of the political areas that it separates, the demarcation retains the austere function of a sentinel, resistant to communication.

This is to a certain degree the case with the frontier between Mexico and the United States. If, on the other hand, no such matching of forces exists, or if for some other reason the frontier loses its conflict potential, it tends to turn into a mere migratory region, prone to the mixing of peoples, languages, and customs, but without stable or genuine solidarity. Then not infrequently it develops into a disordered zone of vice and adventure, like certain slums of great cities. In such cases, the weaker nation tends to suffer humiliations while the other retains the advantages—although not without the latter itself feeling diminished and deprived of its character in that sort of fringe area where the national vitality is exhausted. Frontier zones with a large floating tourist population tend to be particularly exposed to these disordered waves, and this clearly is one of the dangers from which they have to defend themselves if they do not want to see the very foundations of their customs and even of their culture undermined.

But it is not a question only of underscoring these negative potentialities of the settled frontier. Normally the frontier perimeter continues to represent the zone of greatest sensitivity of each people, somewhat as the skin is to the body it envelops. Like the skin of an animal, the frontier serves the human group in maintaining its physical integrity, in absorbing the required energy from the external environment, and even sometimes in expelling its waste products. Though many pernicious influences can insinuate themselves through these boundaries, it is also true that over the dividing line there come to peoples many of the stimuli that keep them from sinking into routine and that spur them to excel.

Not long ago in Spain the great Azorín reminded me that all renascences have been preceded by a breath of fresh air proceeding from the past or from the outside. On the other hand, whenever a people isolated itself within its own confines—China of the Great Wall is the classic example, so is the Spain of the Counter Reformation—it had to nourish itself on its own inner substance and its culture became overspecialized, losing dimensions of variety and universality. It is possible that just this is happening today to the socialist nations isolated by iron curtains.

The Unbalanced Frontier

We have just referred to polemical frontiers and to purely residual ones. It is possible to distinguish still other variations that prove to be applicable to the different types of dividing lines.

The eminent French geographer Jean Brunhes—to whose work I was introduced by our colleague Professor Iñiguez, himself an excellent geographer—distinguishes between "living" and "dead" frontiers. I will express his thought in my own words. Dead frontiers are those across which the electric current of history has ceased to pass. Brunhes cites the Pyrenees as an example. In such cases on neither side of the line are there any great preoccupations, so to speak, even smuggling is looked upon with some leniency. On the other hand, the living frontier is like a high tension cable. The zones that it separates, be they political, economic, or religious, are kept in a belligerent attitude. In the case of states, they live in fear, peering over the line with unconcealed suspicion and, of course, with their weapons at hand. Probably the French geographer was thinking a great deal about the Franco-German frontier as he wrote. Today we could cite as examples the frontier of Israel with the Arab world, and even more conspicuously the far-flung one that carries that enormous charge of electrical potential we call the Cold War.

But there is another distinction—Brunhes does not mention it, as I recall—that equally interests us, especially us Latin Americans, which can be drawn between "balanced" and "unbalanced" frontiers. When a dividing line is fixed, it is often the case that the forces on the two sides are not comparable, since the fixing itself normally results from a disparity of power. When what is now called an "underdeveloped" nation, or simply one endowed with different and more traditional spiritual and cultural resources, is located next to a powerful nation, the frontier is necessarily a source of insecurity and uncertainty for the weaker nation. In the most inert of situations, the frontier completely fails as a means of communication, resulting in arrogance on one side and resentment on the other. The function of the frontier is then limited to preserving as far as possible the respective integrities of the two human groups, both shutting themselves into their corresponding domains. But the usual situation is for the frontier to become a menace, which does not even have to be deliberate. Because of the very disparity between the contiguous forces, the stronger power need not violate the frontier in order to spill over into the neighboring area, and we can even say that it is difficult to avoid doing so.

This spilling over may be only political, but it may be economic as well. It may even be cultural, mainly through psychological means. It may be limited to an influence that is only tacit, but difficult to oppose, or turn into the paternalism of the so-called "spheres of influence," which are, of course, a special prerogative of powerful nations. It may, finally, take the form of penetration by force, which in its most flagrant manifestation we call imperialism. As an index of the power relationships between the two human areas it separates, the frontier is then a crucial zone of incalculable dangers. It tests the intelligence and character with which the weaker of the political, economic, and cultural aggregations bounded by the frontier copes with those perils.

Let me insist that even in those cases where there is no deliberate aggression on the part of the more powerful nation, the mere imbalance of the frontier has a negative effect. The stronger does not trouble itself with the niceties of diplomacy, but instead yields to the temptation to interfere directly or indirectly in a paternal or censorial manner. Moreover, the mere possibility of such spill-over, even if it does not occur, engenders in the subordinate people a kind of chronic resentment that can frustrate or render inefficacious the best intentioned policies that the powerful state might propose.

But we will be better able to speak of all this in connection with the political frontier. Now, in concluding today's task, I should like to add something concerning a special case—that of islands.

The Island Situation

A moment ago we were speaking about isolation. This is then an opportune time to say something about those perfectly encapsulated territories called islands, from which derives the term isolation, with its rather negative connotations. Do islands, because they are islands, have a special repertory of historic possibilities, or a peculiar destiny? Naturally this question is of special interest to us who live on islands; but I cannot stop now to consider it beyond a few hasty considerations as a token of the more complete examination that we will undertake on another occasion.

The matter has tended to stimulate the greatest diversity of reflections. For example, Angel Ganivet in his memorable *Idearium Español,* in developing his thesis about the "territorial spirit," wrote that "continental peoples are characterized by resistance, peninsulars by independence, and islanders by aggression." "The islander," he added, "knows that his isolation is his most reliable defense: He will be able to accept foreign domination if he lacks the power to maintain his independence; but he is in fact independent, and besides, he knows the formative power of his insular land is so potent that if some foreign elements are introduced into it they will not be long in acquiring the feeling of autonomy."

England affords the classic example of this process. The English people's memories of the Norman invasion were obliterated by her defeat of the Invincible Armada. Thenceforth Albion developed an aggressive imperial policy that was able to withstand the test of the Napoleonic threats. Not even the aerial battering of World War II overly disturbed the confidence that Great Britain had accumulated during three centuries, in which the famous "silver thread" of the Channel afforded an invulnerable defense against any danger that might come from the Continent. That state of mind sometimes manifests itself in amusing ways. On a certain occasion when an unusually violent storm struck the English Channel, no less a newspaper than the London *Times* published on the first page a headline that read: "Continent Cut Off By Bad Weather." For that judicious newspaper, England was not involved.

But in the matter of generalizations, others do not turn out to be so optimistic. Thus, for example, your late lamented Antonio Pedreira, in that book of Puerto Rican design bearing the title *Insularity*, of which I treasure a copy the author himself sent me in Cuba, rather seemed inclined to regard insularity as a limitation, above all when it was combined with small physical size. "We bear the mark of territorial size," he wrote. "We are not continentals, nor even Antilleans. We are simply islanders, which is as if to say shut up in a tiny house."

For my part, I do not think the question is to be left to the mercy of any sort of absolute geographical determinism, so much in vogue in the last century. Geography alone does not make history; man creates history in a geographical setting. But it surely makes a great difference whether Mother Earth manifests herself as more or less hospitable. The resources and the obstacles that a territory presents do no more than condition the operation of the human efforts that are expended on it. If anything can be said to determine the destiny of a people, it is the interaction of the one with the other. Probably this is the idea that Pedreira really had in mind, since otherwise he would not have written a book that is apparently so negative but nevertheless is deeply suffused with a confidence in the will of his people that subsequent history has only confirmed.

In purely physical terms, insularity has its benefits and its dangers. An island lacks frontiers in the strictest recognized sense of the word. Ordinarily its entire immediate neighborhood is the sea. In some respects this is a rather unfavorable state of affairs. For example, there is no doubt that Cuba's insularity was, in large measure, the reason she took so much longer to become independent than did the colonies on the mainland. On the other hand, we now see that the terrestrial frontier is almost always what we might call an abrasive surface, on which national temperaments are sharpened. When such a surface is missing, the sea that surrounds the islands makes them more pliant and trustful. But the sea only isolates relatively, and nowadays less than ever. An abundance of coasts and the need for a variety of channels of communication make the island open up wide toward the exterior, as though all of it were potentially a frontier. An island is all pores, and anyone can see that its environment is always more ventilated, in every sense of the word, than that of a continental area whose circumstances in other respects may be analogous. Islands not only receive more diverse influences, but those they receive arrive as though filtered, and without as much impact as they have on terrestrial frontiers.

Of course, all of this can be greatly influenced by the factor of size, and above all by that of location. A large island tends to feel more self-sufficient and projects itself outward more than a small one. It makes no difference whether an island is solitary or forms part of an archipelago, so long as the latter has a sense of its own identity and political integrity, as in the case of a continent. Thus, your noble Hostos* dreamed of an Antilles confederation, which has been unhappily frustrated by the rise of certain historical forces. Finally, it is also a matter of considerable moment whether or not the island is located within the great streams of commerce and whether or not it is more or less close to a center of intense political and economic power. In principle, islands see themselves as less entangled in the life of a neighboring continental mass than do the lands of which the latter is composed. But if the nearby mass is very powerful, the islands find themselves drawn into its vortex, as the floating leaves of a pool swirl around a fountain. In such cases the insular situation commonly engenders a tension similar to that of certain frontiers. To be precise, there arises a true inner frontier of opinion, which often is only latent and at other times may appear with dramatic impact.

But none of this is a matter of necessity. Such geographical realities are one factor in the destiny of an island, but not the decisive factor. Whether or not an island or a constellation of them succeeds in wisely managing these basic conditions depends on the intelligence and character of its people. It is true that sometimes other forces and circumstances also are at work—for example, historical opportunity. I have just recalled this in alluding to the grand vision of Hostos for the Antilles, which came to nought because it arose too late, or perhaps too soon. But even within those great complexes of forces that influence the destiny especially of small peoples, there is a great deal these people can do in the way that counts most, which is to fulfill worthily the historical role that falls to their lot.

---

*Mañach here refers to Eugenio María de Hostos (1839-1903), eminent Puerto Rican essayist and educator, who fostered the idea of cooperation among Spanish-American peoples.—*Tr.*

With this, ladies and gentlemen, we may conclude our introductory considerations about the frontier in general. In the next lecture we shall move on to examine the specific types of frontiers that interest us most. First, we will look at political and economic frontiers, not so much in the abstract, but relating them with the inter-American situation.

II

Political, Ideological, and Economic Frontiers

We devoted our first lecture to certain introductory considerations about frontiers in general, to a biological classification of them, as it were. After trying to determine their common nature, we established certain very general distinctions relating to their hierarchical ordering, more specifically, those between dynamic frontiers, based on conquest, and settled frontiers; and that very important one, for us, between balanced and unbalanced frontiers. We concluded with a reference to the special case of islands, which also directly concerns us. On this foundation, we will begin today to sketch the still more specific types of frontiers that are included within that hierarchy, beginning with political and economic frontiers. These we will not treat as abstractly as we have up to now, but rather view them from the concrete perspective of the American situation.

Just this perspective obliges me to anticipate a certain criticism that may be leveled against all that follows. In applying these generalities to the case of our America, now and again you will note in my exposition and in my arguments certain developments of thought that may seem indecisive, ambivalent, and even occasionally contradictory. I will try to insure that this will be due as little as possible to errors in reasoning. Most of the time it will result from the very reality we are studying. For it happens, in effect, that the real is never as definite, as coherent in its manifestations, and as unequivocal in its meaning as it appears at first sight. The topography of reality is variegated, and like natural landscapes, never presents only a single hue, but a graduated succession of different shades. The judgments we make about things are not only conditioned by their intrinsic

21

complexity, but also by our own varying perspectives. Hence our judgments often turn out to be insufficiently clear, and even ambiguous, if not contradictory. Reality transcends the neat oversimplifications of logic. Perhaps that is why poetry, rather than pure rational judgment, is the best means of grasping it, and why metaphor and paradox are the most adequate tools for translating it into words. It was Goethe, who had a passion both for clarity and profundity, who warned us that thinking is inevitably made up of the conjunction of opposites. True reflection, he said, begins when we say: "Yes . . . but . . . nevertheless . . . "

You will then be able to forgive me if, in what I have to say in the course of these lectures, you do not find those clear-cut judgments and conclusive opinions that so delight the dogmatic demon we all tend to carry around within, but which is not likely to give us anything more than a simplistic and mutilated version of things. It suffices if we shall just be able to penetrate a bit into their complexity.

The Political Frontier

A geographical frontier is nothing more than a line of advance that has become stabilized. After the dynamic phase of peaceful exploration or of conquest by force, the struggle for territory more or less definitely stops. What determines where the line is fixed?

No doubt sometimes it is simply a matter of geographical accident, such as the barrier of a mountain chain or the basin of a great river. But except in the relatively distant past, when the disproportion of human and natural forces was clearly much greater, that factor has not generally been the most decisive one. In general, geography does not make history; it is man who creates history within geography. Although he may take advantage of geographical accident for the purpose of *demarcating* his territorial gains, normally there are other causes and circumstances that set a limit to them: the exhaustion of the expansive impulse in the face of the opposing resistance; estimates of strategic or economic sufficiency, and particularly considerations about "rounding out" the national territory or reuniting scattered parts of the same racial group within the same political framework; and finally, on occasion, international settlements like those that set and upset the frontiers of Poland for two centuries. It is common knowledge that such settlements are not customarily made in response to historical considerations, but rather to the blind play of political interests, notably to what is called the "balance of power," which is an exclusive affair of the big nations.

The matter of rounding out the national territory deserves particular attention. The criterion governing it and the limits it may have also pertain to the secret of pure power—*arcana imperii*. Rarely is it supported by considerations that might be recognized as objectively valid, such as that of assuring channels of communication or points of access indispensable for the national life. For the most part, the effort is made in response to a purely subjective and unwarranted vision of size, well-roundedness, and geographical completeness. An example of this is the long-standing North American idea of carrying the frontiers of the United States to the gulf, if not to the isthmus. Nothing else was behind the Jeffersonian doctrine of manifest destiny, which contributed so largely to curtailing the much more genuine and patent destiny of our Antilles. On the other hand, no less arbitrary is the pretext that has been and is still used to create buffer states, with which frontiers are extended, and which often get incorporated into larger states at the smallers' expense. Thus we conclude that the fixing of the frontier is almost always a purely arbitrary exercise of naked power.

Nevertheless, even in this matter the conscience of the world is able to do something and has been doing something. Presently we will see that in the final determination of our frontier with the United States, and in her behavior in relation to it, weight was given to considerations other than the most concrete interests of that country—inhibitions and restraints of a certain ethico-political type, growing out of the very evolution of the North American spirit. This is clearly an example of the ambivalence-producing developments with which historical reality presents us. Although an oversimplistic realism constantly tempts us to adopt a cynical explanation of history—"expect evil and you will find it"—it is also true that sometimes its movements result from motivations that, for want of a better word, we may call ideals.

Whatever may be the motivations and the forces at work, from their push and pull emerge the frontiers that are most genuinely political. The geographer Brunhes, in his book *The Geography of History,* expressed the function of these boundaries very clearly, though perhaps in an oversimplified way. "Collective security," he said, "the essential goal of political societies, is not realized until the state is capable of insuring the inner cohesion of its component parts and of establishing on its periphery a permanent framework for its defense. These are two distinct functions, each with its appropriate geographical expression: the *road* for the first, the *frontier* for the second."

It follows that the political frontier is not merely the physical boundary of the nation and an expression of political power but also an index of collective consciousness and vigor. People without national cohesiveness or without a sense of historic vocation, people indifferent to their destiny, in fact do not usually care much about having good highways to join them together, nor stable frontiers to separate and protect them from those outside. To the degree that peoples become strong and conscious of themselves and develop a yearning for prestige, they proceed to impose and make definite their boundaries, often by violence and in opposition to the obstacles of physical nature. This has occurred in most of the continental nations of Latin America.

Like the separate space of one's own house, the political frontier represents the domain of higher domesticity that we call the fatherland and that Martí defined as "the part of humanity in which it was our lot to be born." In relation to it, the function of the frontier is not just that of defense, as Brunhes says, but also that of preserving one's own traditions and values, without detriment to communication with the outside world. If in former times the frontier could be likened to the moat of a castle, in modern times, as a result of the greater efficacy of military techniques, the defensive function has increasingly subordinated itself to that of simple national delineation, and in a more concrete sense, to that of commercial and cultural communication.

In principle, the internal values that the frontier is called upon to protect are those of the people's own historic physiognomy, and on the individual plane, those of liberty and security. Unfortunately, in the life of nations, pathological crises sometimes occur, in which one if not all of those functions fails and the frontier is transformed into a ring of iron that stifles the nation and the citizens within it. Then what a different meaning familiar actions and words assume! "To reach the frontier" is the ultimate goal of the persecuted. When they are not mere delinquents in flight, but rebels with honor, the freedom and the security they acquire at the frontier is that of being able to advocate their own ideas—particularly ideas about the collective destiny, though it be at the cost of exile.

But that is a dismal recourse. Every exile, voluntary or otherwise, is felt as a wound in the soul—a wound to which the frontier applies the first bandage. Locke said that the number of exiles of a nation is an indication of the extent to which its people are ruled by their own desires. The judgment is valid at least for political emigrés. How unfortunate are the peoples who see the number of their outlaws mount! On the other hand, as fortunate as they are generous are those who, through the freedom of their institutions, unreservedly open their doors to the exiles!

In relation to the world outside, the frontier normally is a symbol of national dignity. I recalled earlier that the word with which it is designated comes from "front"*—surely a noble and prolific term, seeing that it has sired a whole line of lively expressions such as "to put up a bold front," "to confront," "to front toward," "to have a false front," and "to affront." In the human body, the front (in the sense of forehead) is the most noble part of the countenance and that in which we seem to feel, along with the bubbling of ideas, the conscientious constraints of honor that rise from the core of our being. We care for our front (the appearance we make) like a polished medal, preserving it from tarnish, exposed as it is to accidents and misfortunes. We all know what ugly meanings the malicious world in some cases attributes to it. When Clemenceau discovered that one of his generals commanding the front in Salonica, a man well along in years, had married a young girl, he let loose one of his witty ejaculations: *"Est-ce qu'il veut avoir deux fronts a défendre?"*—"Does he want to have two fronts to defend?"

Thus the frontier is also that part of the general "hide" of the nation—or group of nations—that is most ostensibly associated with the collective honor. It seems to be a mirror of the people's soul, where its countenance comes into focus. It is where the people shows itself most sensitive to an affront or an unfriendly smile, where its frown betrays resentment, and, in its serenity, its enjoyment of other's respect.

Political communities are accustomed to tolerate many things in the recesses of their own being; what they cannot resign themselves to without humiliation is to "lose face."

Consequently international relations normally avail themselves of something more than pure force, imposing on themselves prudential considerations that reflect a sense of limits, in those polite conventions that nations adhere to even when they knit an eyebrow. Diplomatic courtesies, extraterritoriality—which we Hispanic Americans have carried to the sometimes excessive refinement of the right of exile—and respect for agreements and treaties are some of the other manifestations of this international formality.

The frontier is in part the symbol of such civilities. For this reason, so-called "frontier incidents," even when least deliberate and tangible, are so very painful to the nation's sensibility. "Frontier violations" are even more painful and rarely forgotten, and I would

---

*Here Mañach comments on a variety of idiomatic expressions deriving from the Spanish *frente*—'front.' The English derivations are not as numerous nor do they generally parallel those of the Spanish. The translated sentences that follow thus necessarily fall short of expressing the intention of the Spanish original.—*Tr.*

say that they hurt most when they show the least deliberation. An invasion, for example, like a personal physical attack, presupposes a certain kind of consideration, even though it be hostile. It is an act by means of which one state is so concerned about another that it wishes to subdue it by force. But the violation of a frontier through mere oversight is a lack of consideration, a discounting of the other personality, supposing it sensitive only to violent and crude attacks.

Frontier and Sovereignty

Closely related to the above is a problem that merits special consideration, though its summary treatment here will be out of proportion to its importance. I refer to the difficult problem of sovereignty, and particularly to that of the admissible limitation on the independence of states and therefore on the absolute nature of the political frontier.

As is well known, the classical doctrine has traditionally maintained that sovereignty is an absolute value and right. It could be infringed in fact, but not by right. When the former occurred, it was always by virtue of an aggressive cynicism, and never happened without causing a scandal both in powerful nations capable of the same sin, and even more so in weak ones, for whom sovereignty was to be regarded as an invulnerable shield. With the evolution of the ideas of human solidarity, and above all with the development of a different order of interests that have accentuated the interaction of peoples, this doctrine has been undergoing modifications. First in a positive sense: While maintaining their sovereignty, nations find it convenient to cooperate with one another to gain advantages or to avoid dangers that affect all, even though to do so they must enter into agreements that to some degree affect their sovereignty. Then from a negative angle: Independence cannot be carried to the extreme of permitting a nation to violate human interests within or beyond its borders, and if it does, it has no right to appeal to sovereignty to protect itself from the possible intervention of other nations or states.

These modifications, which up to World War I had scarcely reached the level of doctrine, in recent times have steadily been advancing more definitely to the positive plane of political action, sometimes by virtue of agreements among groups of nations, but principally by means of international instrumentalities of which the United Nations is the archetype. As an example of their application it suffices to mention the case of the Congo.

Needless to say, the utility of this new political philosophy for resolving or averting conflicts of interest among nations is at the same time a source of danger, particularly for weak nations, the only ones on whom the limitation of sovereignty really can have any effect. Once the possible legitimacy of foreign intervention in the internal affairs of any nation has been granted, the flexibility of the principle can get out of bounds and lend itself to all sorts of conniving.

If there be any solution to so ticklish a problem, it must be that of combining a fundamental principle with a procedural norm. I believe the former is to be sought at the level of the highest interests common to all peoples. Among the values of the historical and public realm, as among those of the private domain, there is a clear hierarchy. This order is not established arbitrarily but by the tacit consensus of humanity—although it is frequently unrecognized or subverted. And too, the highest values still have no adequate organized protection, as in the case of the so-called human rights. What is required is to make such protection viable. Among civilized peoples, primacy must be accorded the specific values to which these rights refer: liberty, justice, and respect both for other people and for the civilized order itself. The other order, the purely mechanical one of docility to the public power and of no visible disturbance to the peace, is only of accessory value. It is valuable only to the degree that it guarantees the substantive values, on which any security worthy of the name clearly depends.

The recognition of this hierarchy of public values and the political means needed to make it effective is, in the final analysis, what has come in our day to devalue the concept of sovereignty, stripping it of the absolute character that had been attributed to it in classical theorizing. The experience of the last fifty years has taught us that the human must take precedence over the national; that in politics as in economics peoples affect one another and frequently depend on one another, and that no government truly represents its people when it enthrones arbitrariness and oppression on its own soil. The political frontier must be the shield of the collective dignity, never a fence to keep the people in subjection.

How far such criteria of an ethico-political order can be made to apply in practice without lending themselves to distortion and misuse is still another question. At present, obviously, the scope of their application is still very limited. It will continue to be so as long as there exist suspicions and competitions for power among the very nations that, because of their importance or their maturity and prestige, would be expected to serve as guardians of those principles. In any event, the sole possible guarantee of such interventionism in the face of the misuse of sovereignty apparently must be found in international collaboration. It is always dangerous to set up a single nation as arbiter of the destiny of others. Unfortunately, the principles of public rights have not yet achieved anything like the objectivity with which the standards of private rights are vested. This is shown by the single fact that a revolution is considered a source of rights simply by virtue of having been consummated in fact. In the absence of objective bases for making value judgments in the public domain, there only remains the consensus of opinion. It is worth remarking that in the face of a national situation of flagrant arbitrariness, brutally injurious to the most obvious human rights, the only wise recourse seems to be that of multilateral intervention on the basis of prior unanimous collective agreement among the states in the immediate geographic and historic neighborhood.

The United States and Ourselves

But it is now time to take the generalities we have expounded—and their possible exceptions—and apply them to what most interests us: our frontier with the United States and the relationships that it represents. You certainly will already have seen these alluded to in some of what I have pointed out. Nevertheless, not everything negative in the foregoing generalities is applicable to our powerful neighbor. In some cases she might rather be a good example of the opposite.

Before I go on to explain, it will be well to make a personal declaration. I have not come here to exonerate anyone for anything. I will have plenty to say about our great North American neighbor in these lectures. I will try to do it with objectivity and always with sincerity, and when appropriate, with severity or with praise. I believe that estimates of the United States in general, and of its actions in the past fifty years in particular, have been shot through with stereotypic judgments and crude simplifications. Of course, those who deceive themselves in this way are the first to suffer, among other reasons because the deliberate despising of others creates havoc with one's judgments concerning the worth of what is one's own.

Let us begin with the very establishment of our frontier with the United States.

The decline of Spain as a world power began in the seventeenth century. It coincided with the rise in North America of another more deliberate and vigorous will to empire. The latter first employed its energies in the expansion of its initial holdings, that is to say, in advancing the frontier. In this undertaking it developed an aggressive fighting spirit, a zest for risk and adventure, a confidence in its own powers, and a habit of personal liberty. All of these it later used against the founding power in the struggle of the colonies for independence. Once that enterprise was completed, the United States conceived the purpose of rounding out its territory. The weakness of Spain and the opportunism of Napoleon initially assisted this effort. But that was not enough. Jefferson then spoke of manifest destiny, and it was not known whether the expansion he contemplated would reach to the isthmus that so clearly links the two great divisions of the continent. In order to achieve that dominion, the United States had to have a free hand. The European powers were not to block it. Then Monroe traced—albeit only theoretically—the most vast frontier the world had hitherto known. A few thrusts of the claw stripped Mexico of a third of her territory. In the American history text I studied as a boy it was said in all sincerity that this had been simply the bullying of a weak nation by another of greater power and few scruples.

The matter did not stop there. During the remainder of the century Central America also suffered invasions and more or less official threats. In 1881, Joseph R. Hawley, a United States senator, asked euphorically at a political banquet: "And when we have taken Canada and Mexico and rule over the Continent without rivals, what type of civilization shall we come to have in the future?" Martí, who was then in the United States, replied to him in one of his dispatches to a newspaper in Venezuela: "A dreadful one, in truth: that of Carthage!" It is not strange, then, that from that time forward, the Cuban apostle accelerated the struggle for the independence of Cuba and Puerto Rico. Thirteen years later, on the eve of his heroic death, he confided to his Mexican friend Manuel Mercado the most fundamental motive of his liberating zeal: to impede "the extension of the United States into the Antilles and its falling on our American territories with that much more power."

We all know the outcome of United States strategy. For Cuba, it meant an independence that the Platt Amendment* for a long time made essentially nominal. For Puerto Rico, like the Philippines, it meant only a change of masters—but the new one was a stranger to the language, the traditions, and the customs of the country. Not only was the political destiny of the island compromised, but its cultural destiny was as well. To this we will return later.

I have introduced this as an example of deliberate and almost methodical imperialist expansion; but also to follow it with the question of why this expansion came to a halt precisely in our Antilles, thus manifesting a certain restraint, as if not desiring to reach the

---

*An act of the U.S. Congress under which Cuba, though independent in name, was in effect a protectorate of the United States from 1902 until 1934.—*Tr.*

point of completely blotting out our free will. It is true that later were to come the Panama episode and still later those in the Dominican Republic and Guatemala. But these were just that: episodes, and now with motivations very different from the pure eagerness for expansion. Moreover, the subsequent behavior of the United States in relation to Cuba, to the Philippines, and to Puerto Rico itself, was such as to make credible the position that not even its outreach over these islands was in response to a true will to empire. The Philippines are completely free; the pressure of the Platt Amendment was withdrawn from Cuba; Puerto Rico is now a "free associated state," and will have its independence the day it wants it.

I have no doubt that calculations of the so-called realists may have had weight in this restraint by the United States. For example, did it feel its political, economic, and strategic influence in the Caribbean area was by then sufficient? But I wonder if in the same circumstances other powerful nations would have been content with that. And when I relate this conduct to what the United States has subsequently been working out in the international domain, I arrive at the conclusion that—together with egoistic motivations of national interest—certain considerations of an ethical and democratic order have been operating, in which one can see the reappearance on a larger scale of those characteristic features that Santayana ascribed to the Puritan tradition.

After all, nations are made up of people, and democracies are those civico-political environments where public opinion counts and with it the feelings, the constraints, and the sense of justice of the citizens. The United States is not the only example of this. We have seen how France, faced with the problem of Algeria, put itself in a position of making maximum concessions. Considering the importance of the colonial interests involved, not all of a material nature, I do not believe that the force of the Algerian insurrection would have sufficed for the actual outcome. I think it is due instead to the opinion of its most enlightened citizenry, which led France to exalt the intimations of its own conscience over calculations of self-interest and self-regard. Such contrition is generally only within the capacity of free regimes. One of the most terrible corruptions of totalitarianisms is that, by fostering in the people the primal instincts of nationalism and violence, their generous impulses are stifled.

Returning to the United States, we observe the dual realistic-idealistic polarity of its politics that makes it sometimes appear at fault in its external relations. Such is the case in connection with manifestly reprehensible Latin American political situations. The nation most relied upon in the world for the defense of freedom seems indifferent—if not acquiescent—to the existence of oppressive governments in our republics. I believe that this is due to two causes, one material and the other formal. The first consists in Washington's tendency to not have much confidence in our countries' capacity for democratic living, which an English author many years ago saw as inexorably subject to a pendular oscillation between despotism and anarchy. Put in the position of having to suffer through one or the other of these, the United States sees itself led by its own economic interests, and sometimes by those of the international political system, to compromise with excesses of authority. In saying this I have no intention of justifying that attitude. It has been demonstrated time and again that this premise of dilemma-producing pendularity is false. What our republics are really subject to is circular or reciprocal betrayal involving limited social development and political corruption, conditions that favor one another. But it would be well to pay more attention to the majority of our republics that are now breaking that vicious circle through a democratic effort that is extremely difficult because it presupposes the necessity of using limited power to correct the conditions that conspire against it.

What I have called the formal cause of the attitude of the United States toward oppressive dictatorships is the principle of nonintervention, adopted at the instance of the other American nations themselves. Entirely sound in theory, this principle may nevertheless be counterproductive in practice. As for the United States, the weight of its mere presence on the American scene is such that even when Washington may have been very careful about abstention—and it is not always so—the mere attitude of passivity or diplomatic circumspection *vis-à-vis* the oppressive governments is virtually equivalent to backing them. Hence, in spite of the principle of nonintervention having been adopted in inter-American conferences, it is frequently the Latin American democratic elements themselves, injured by such regimes, who petition the United States for pressure in defense of common ideals. This, then, is how a conflict between principle and reality arises.

If there is any solution to this intricate problem, which involves such diverse factors as nationalistic zeal, political prudence, and historical responsibility, I think it is to be sought on the level of the highest interests common to all nations, and to ours in particular.

The Peril of Imperialism

With all of this we have been coming closer to the problem of imperialism, the most insidious danger that hangs over the unbalanced frontier. The topic is shot through with nonsense, sometimes quite calculated and calculating, as we all know. It would be desirable sometime to examine it calmly, and of course with more time than we have at our disposal.

Naturally, it will not occur to anyone to deny that in the political order there has always existed and there still exists, with new and more perilous variations, a type of *deliberate* imperialism, the only kind to which the term really applies. It consists in projecting the will to dominion of one nation over another. But I believe that among the democratic nations we have made some progress toward containing these expansive movements, which in large measure were generated from the disparity in the rates of progress of the various nations. Just as this disparity resulted in the elaboration of the theory of "the civilized man's responsibility," so also it gave a motive, or sometimes no more than a pretext, for the powerful nations imposing themselves on the weak ones. But this classical imperialism today is definitely in bad repute, just like its counterpart, colonialism. The archetypical British Empire now is more shadow than substance, and all of its type that still remain are on the defensive and their days are numbered.

I insist that I am referring to the imperialism of *democratic* nations. In their case the reason is clear. No form of conduct continues to exist if it is contrary to the principles that sustain it. In the Western world, democracy has made headway—if not always as a living reality, at least as the preferred way of life. And this way is based, as we all know, on the plurality of vigorously held opinions and on government by the express consent of the governed. Democracy thus cannot be intrinsically—I emphasize the word—imperialist. Often it has permitted and still permits such violence, but not without first having done violence to its own conscience.

On the other hand, totalitarian regimes—whether called fascism or communism—feel a congenital need to dominate. Imbued with doctrines whose inculcation would automatically oppose the spontaneous and deepset inclinations of the human spirit, they see themselves obliged to impose these doctrines on the domestic scene by violence, and then they do not feel secure unless everybody in the outside world also shares them. So they forcibly subject neighboring nations and deceive the rest by claiming technical and social achievements that, though often authentic and even admirable, are obtained through an enormous concentration of material power and at the price of enslaving the governed. In this way such regimes put together a fanatical "mystique" and an unscrupulous political strategy, both of which are ingredients of a new brand of imperialism, much more implacable and ominous than that of the democratic nations with which they pretend to equate it.

In the face of this, democracy has unfortunately not yet found the formula for the only totalitarianism that would be permissible for it: that of impregnating all of society with its advantages. There are too many disparities of fortune not determined by aptitude or by effort, too many forms of waste and disorder, too many falsehoods that cry to heaven for redress. It is owing to its uneasy conscience about all this that democracy has not been able to elaborate its own mystique, that is, a sufficiently ardent self-awareness and a strong capacity for proselytizing. Finally, its own integrity and ideological conclusions conspire against such a mystique, since it feels itself obliged to respect the free dissemination of the very doctrines that aim to destroy it. Of all this, its enemies take advantage.

The Ideological Frontier

This would be a good occasion on which to include in our examination an appropriate meditation on the greatest and most dramatic frontier that divides the world today—the ideological frontier. But it is obvious that, aside from the other limitations I suffer from, the importance and the breadth of this topic demand more space than I have at my disposal. I shall limit myself to a few very summary reflections simply by way of suggestion.

First, it is highly unfortunate that the present conflict is formulated as a disjunction between "capitalism" and "communism." With this alone the enemies of Western democracy have already won half the battle in the average person's mind. For capitalism is an antipathetic word, as is—if we are to be psychologically realistic—the phrase and even the concept of private property. Both expressions and both institutions betray a privacy and exclusiveness that provoke the resentment of the majority of people, who are without fortune and property. On the other hand communism, going back to the Golden Age referred to earlier, has had pleasing, generous, and "human" connotations.

Strictly speaking, the distinction between the two systems is much more profound. It has to do with the development of Western civilization since the industrial revolution. This civilization has been marked by a technical orientation that sought to compensate for its basic materialism through certain ingredients of residual Christian religiosity that were strong enough to sustain the ultimate worth of the person by reference to life's spiritual dimension. With these ingredients were also associated a psychological corollary: freedom as a condition for personality; and a social corollary: private property as a condition for personal independence and its development. Moreover, such connections were not gratuitous. In the last analysis they were based on a transcendent conception of man and of life.

For this religious transcendence, Marxism substituted historical transcendence or, if you will, an immanentist conception. It sought the salvation of man on earth, not in the life beyond. With society thus reduced to its purely economic base, man saw himself deprived of his spiritual destiny and converted into a piece of the social machine itself. And since what is most concrete and decisive about that machine is the material power that moves it, that is, the labor of man, all social efficacy was reduced to the organization and distribution of that power. Property was also dissociated from the person, passing to the domain of the state. Thus all of the mechanisms of society came to concentrate themselves on the control of the means of production. Spiritual values, such as those of culture and morality, passed into the superstructure of the economic mechanism. In order to assure the supremacy of the latter, every other ethical value associated with the person could be and had to be implacably suppressed.

If this analysis is correct, what it makes clear is that the entire opposition between liberal democracy and so-called social democracy revolves around this dilemma of transcendence and immanence, which in the last analysis has been the great dilemma of Western culture ever since the Renaissance. Thus it is true to say that we are faced with the crisis of an epoch. What must be the resolution of this conflict?

I do not think it consists in a violent clash. If history teaches us anything—and I belong to those who think it teaches a great deal, even though it may not repeat itself—it is that no great idea for human betterment has ever perished nor been able to be suppressed. It did not happen to Christianity, nor to Renaissance humanism, nor to the liberalism of the great Western revolutions, nor to the materialism of the industrial revolution. Nor will it happen to the socialist idea. But history also shows that none of these great mutations has brought about a total substitution of values. The advance of humanity absorbs all innovations, but does so by incorporating them into its own accumulated substance, that is, without giving up the important gains already achieved.

Freedom is one of these gains. Benedetto Croce did not exaggerate too much in saying that history is "the saga of freedom," of the expansion of the human spirit. It is the source of all the progress that man has made down the centuries in dignity, in culture, and in well-being. It would be absurd to insist on giving up freedom on account of the delay in realizing it fully. But on the other hand, there stands as a challenge, as a temptation that is very seductive to many, the socialist idea of a world less entrusted to purely individual caprice and interest, more rooted in the rights of all, in security, in efficiency, in the elimination of the rivalries that create violence and war, and more dedicated to the utilization of technical knowledge and skill. It would be foolish to deny that this ideology is making gigantic strides forward or to characterize as defeatist the certainty many of us have that Western democracy now lacks sufficient power to impose itself unilaterally by any form of persuasion, of proselytism, or of politics. On the other hand, the resolution of the conflict cannot consist in a violent clash, which would be no solution but rather a dissolution of everything in the civilized order and possibly the destruction of the world. There remains only the possibility of conciliation. But is this really possible between such radically antagonistic philosophies?

I do not believe it is, since I have already said that between the two runs the opposition of the transcendent and the immanent, which is an eternal tension in man. But I do believe in the possibility of a coexistence that in the long run may turn out to be productive. Today this word coexistence has hypocritical connotations. But it is possible that the reality itself, the balancing of the forces in conflict, will in the end make it an expression of sincerity. The primary condition for such coexistence, then, would be the maintenance of the two forces at their maximum strength. It is possible that if both poles are convinced that the destruction of one by the other is impossible, they will end up becoming conscious of the crime against humanity that is entailed in using so much spiritual energy and so much money in military preparedness, which would by themselves be sufficient to resolve all social problems. This would then be the prelude to a new era in which these rival philosophies would mutually modify one another, democracy becoming even more socialized and socialism becoming more liberal, but preserving sufficient independence so that both would have the opportunity of showing which is the most promising for the happiness and dignity of man. Finally I believe that, with the advent of new generations less inflamed by doctrinal polemics, at last the commitment to universality that I mentioned earlier will assert itself as the great central current flowing through history.

But this optimistic digression has taken us too far afield from the immediate and real problem that concerns us today. On the level of generalities we still have something to say about the economic frontier.

The Economic Frontier

If the definition we initially gave of the frontier in general is valid, this next variant presupposes a contradiction or at least an opposition of material interests—interests of production, of distribution, and of exchange—between territorial areas more or less contiguous, as for example, England and the European Continent, or to come to the case at hand, the United States and our America. When it is a matter of nations equally favored by nature and by their historical development, this relation is simply a form of competition, similar to that which is established among individual enterprises. And, like these, it remains subject to one of two alternatives: the classical one, of absolute freedom of participation and "every man for himself," or, on the other hand, a mutual understanding for the best utilization of each one's energies. As we know, this is the tendency at present, represented by agreements such as those of the Common Market and other analogous ones.

When it is a matter of countries or groups of countries with very different economies by virtue of their natural characteristics, as happens between industrial areas and areas with raw materials, the only alternative to unilateral domination or to intergroup anarchy has to be based on the mechanisms of specialization and compensation. The former aim at granting to each country preference in the production, and possibly in the distribution, of those products for which it is especially well endowed to produce by nature itself or by its own historical development. Such preference, though, ought not to extend to the extreme of suppressing all the incentives for economic diversification that might be within reach. The mechanisms of compensation are those that operate in such a way as to assure, for example, comparability between the prices of the industrial products of one country and the agricultural products of others. In Latin America, the adoption of such mechanisms, as well as the establishment of common markets, if a layman's opinion is valid, would suffice to promote greater prosperity for our countries and assure the stability of hemispheric commercial relations. Though political penetration across a frontier is wont to carry economic penetration along with it, such a linkage is not as inevitable as some would have us believe, and in any case, the intelligent thing is to prevent both at the same time.

Nevertheless, it must not be forgotten that the economic factor tends of its own nature to be expansive. It consists, of course, in producing and distributing and in buying and selling, which presuppose external connections, ample planning, and the search for raw materials and for markets with purchasing power, wherever they may be found. Neither classical capitalism nor communistic capitalism—for the latter also exists, though only in the hands of the state—recognizes frontiers, and incidentally, this economic rivalry, as much as or more than purely ideological differences, is what underlies the present conflict of the superpowers. The statesmen and economists with the broadest vision agree that one of the causes—perhaps the major one—of the world's present malaise is the tension or disparity between the natural expansiveness of the economic factor and the resistance of the political factor, which tends to be principally centripetal and nationalistic.

When political pressure follows economic pressure, it is only through a certain crudeness in planning or procedures, as occurred in America when the flag of the United States, assisted by the "big stick" of Theodore Roosevelt, followed the investor's dollar. It was a deliberate economic imperialism, of which it seems the United States has repented, and properly so. From the time of the second Roosevelt down to the present—with the possible exception of the case of Guatemala, in which the interests of the United Fruit Company were mixed with other things now clearly seen, such as communist interference—what is still called economic imperialism over our countries has been for the most part something quite different. It is not a question of thrusting forth an exploitative will, but of a strong, overabundant, highly industrialized economy spreading out over areas whose meager capacity for industrialization—combined, let us admit it, with disunity and inertia—keeps them reduced to the position of being almost exclusively producers of raw materials. In adventuring into such zones, which are generally very disturbed by local politics, the surplus capital of the North tends to procure for itself unusually large profit margins to compensate for the risks assumed, and hence the exploitative appearance that these investments frequently take on. When this constitutes something more than an appearance, the abuses that accompany it are inexcusable. But it would be salutary also to appreciate how fruitful and stimulating this economic outreach can be, and most frequently is, for the nations whose natural resources it promotes.

In any event, we can always do much to prevent irrigation from becoming destruction. The recent Caribbean Conference, carried out under the auspices of this university, heard the following words from my good Colombian friend Germán Arciniegas:

> In the life of the continent, an unmoving frontier has been demarcated. This frontier is the one that marks where the industrial world of the North ends and where the raw material South begins. This frontier is beginning to disappear, it is

true, although a bit late. But while some of it remains, there
will be a discontinuity across which peoples thrust themselves and politics overflows.

There is a great deal of truth in this. But I wonder if it would not
serve Arciniegas's own thought to invert his argument: as long as
the discontinuity exists, we will have a frontier exposed to overrun-
ning, both political and economic. In large measure it is up to us to
prevent it, as the eminent Argentine authority Raúl Prebisch also
suggested here not long ago. From our side of the unbalanced frontier, we can exert greater pressure of economic activity, studying our
natural resources, adopting modern techniques and habits of saving,
integrating markets, installing internal systems for the distribution
and diversification of agrarian property, and industrializing ourselves. And above all, imposing on ourselves soundly democratic
forms of social and political discipline.

The Frontier and Our Commitment

Some time ago, in a certain international congress of democratic
intellectuals that took place in a European city, a number of Latin
Americans were conversing, and it still pains me to recall the com-
plaining attitude of practically all of them. On returning from the
congress I read in a British journal a comment on this very point.
"The Latin Americans," said the English writer, "tried, as usual, to
export their responsibilities."

A hard saying, for sure! Hard and perhaps not wholly fair. But
let us agree that it had a certain modicum of truth. In the face of the
pressures of a political and economic order to which our unbalanced
frontier is exposed, in addition to this attitude of evasive complaint
that consists in throwing all the blame on the neighbor, there are
also two extreme types of reaction: one, a certain surly, resentful
antagonism to the neighbor's power and one's own impotence; the
other, the contrary and still worse attitude, a cowardly submission,
which sometimes becomes conniving activity and which in political
jargon is generally called a "sellout."

Between these two extremes there is a mode of conduct of which
we countries most directly on the frontier are particularly called to
be an example. It is simply the attitude, or better, the *action* of being
discerning and creative: one that makes a virtue of necessity itself
and of limitation, a stimulus; one that does not weary of proposing
and pursuing high objectives, nor of accumulating the energy and
the high resolve to serve them; and finally, one that does not exclude
nor imitate, but which exerts itself to excel.

Let us make every effort to outdo ourselves organizing in this way, taking fullest advantage of our spiritual and material resources, which are many, and effectively cooperating with one another, which is the most reliable means of strengthening ourselves individually as nations. After all, what right do we have to protest against the northern frontier, or the violations of it, if we do not ourselves finish the job of erasing the frontiers between ourselves, or at least of reducing them to simple geography? How will we be able to face up squarely to the United States to the degree that may be necessary if we insist on continuing to be what Salvador de Madariaga called "the Disunited States of America"? The day on which, having made every effort, we should find that it had been in vain, we would have a reason for talking about insuperable misfortunes, and about obstinate political and economic forces. But what I now see in view is a very different prospect. The world is moving against all abdications, imbalances, and apathies. The more we understand how to adjust the rhythm of our efforts to this contemporary movement, the sooner we will succeed in balancing the frontier for the benefit of all Americans: now the political and economic frontier, but also the cultural frontier, about which we will speak in what follows.

III

The Cultural

Frontier

In the last lecture I tried to set forth certain general concepts in preparation for the inquiry that we launch today, which is that of the cultural frontier. I trust that I am not overly optimistic in thinking that in the dialogue that every lecture establishes between the word of him who speaks and the look of those who listen, on some essential matters we are in agreement. One of these is that since every frontier is a situation involving relationships of both contiguity and opposition between two spheres of interest, and since the interests may be of greater or lesser weight, there exists a hierarchy of frontiers determined by the importance of these interests and the purposes they involve. In this scale, the political and the economic frontiers, which we have examined in a cursory way, occupy a lower level than the cultural frontier, since what confront one another on the latter are entire modes of life, ways of thinking, feeling, and acting, and systems of values.

All of this is, in fact, what we refer to as "culture." You will agree with me, however, that this concept, in spite of having been much studied, still remains confused. I believe that in large part this is due to using the same word to cover too many things.

Culture and its Dimensions

Anthropologists use the word culture, as we know, to designate the particular way of life that distinguishes any human aggregate, no matter how primitive, and thus they speak, for example, of Central African or Polynesian cultures. This use of the plural indicates that it is not a question of anything absolute or universal, but at the most, one of the local forms in which the very general abstraction of a way of life is concretized and diversified. Such forms are primordial, particular, and spontaneous. The customs, the basic social or-

40

ganization, the magical and religious beliefs and practices, are all features that are conserved by the self-perpetuation of the tradition, without deliberation or cultivation—by a way that we might speak of as untamed. Even with respect to beliefs, the element of spirituality in these cultures is minimal, bordering on the purely animal, and thus their human dimension is also minimal. Of course, for peoples in such a social state, their distinctive forms of life are an object of their preference and esteem, and therefore constitute "values." But it is a question of relative, particular values. In this anthropological sense, the word culture connotes a dominant idea of *peculiarity*.

In another extreme and opposite sense, the same word is employed to designate what we sometimes call high culture. This is the highest spiritual activity of a civilized people, of a people who have come to govern themselves by standards and values of special efficacy for social conduct and even for life itself. Nevertheless, civilization is not the same as culture in the superior sense of which I am now speaking. The latter presupposes the cultivation and fulfillment of the noblest aspirations of man as a being with reason, with conscience, and with sensitivity. This culture, therefore, is the elaboration of values that for that very reason are—or deserve to be—the object of universal approval. In this sense, culture does not signify something that is, but something one has. It does not refer to the collective and basic characteristics of a human group that is internally very homogeneous—though generally quite different from others— but to a spiritual attitude, necessarily of a minority, that nevertheless is characterized by its concern for *universality*.

Well now, it is evident that such extreme levels are not the only ones there are. Between them is a middle level, on which culture is neither a basic condition nor a refined activity, but the general mode of behavior of a civilized society. It may maintain residual elements of a primitive stage, but it unites them with the values of "civilization" to which I referred before. These values are concerned with conduct in general, with the most effective relationships of man with man and with nature, with standards of coexistence, with conveniences and techniques. And to these it adds religious, moral, and aesthetic values formed in its own historical experience and elaborated by the educated minority or derived from the example of others. Culture understood in this sense is usually simply called civilization.

Of course this three-dimensional scheme involves the oversimplification inevitable in every attempt of this kind. The levels of which I speak do not necessarily correspond to societies of a distinct type, but may be and generally are, internal dimensions of a given society. Only primitive communities exhibit just the first dimension, the purely anthropological one, and no society, not even among the most advanced, can be said to have completely attained the highest level, that is, of being totally a fulfillment of high culture. It is generally the case that in one and the same people of any given time, and well along in their evolution, there are segments of society situated on different cultural levels. Today, for example, there are cases —the nearest would be found in our own Latin America—that exhibit, on top of a mass that is still primitive, a half-civilized class, and a minority that is the flower of sensitivity and thought.

What for simplicity we are calling the cultural frontier, that is the frontier *between cultures,* is also an ambiguous concept. It can be understood as a dividing line or a zone between physical areas with different cultures, as happens when we speak of the Franco-German cultural frontier, or metaphorically as the contrast between two cultures that in some fashion are opposed and related in our thought, though they may not share any geographical contiguity. Thus we speak of the frontier between Islam and Christianity, or between East and West. Strictly speaking, we ought to reserve this concept for the first of these interpretations, in which the cultural confrontation is produced not by virtue of a simple comparison we make, but as a result of an objective situation: geographical tangency.

With equal concern for precision, we can say that such a cultural frontier exists only with respect to what we have called the middle culture. To be sure, primitive cultures having their own perimeters can differ greatly among themselves, and their respective domains may on occasion impinge on one another, giving rise to violent struggles. But perhaps it would be too much to honor those boundaries with the name cultural frontiers. We have just seen that the frontier is essentially a creation of historical consciousness.

On the other hand, if we consider high culture, the very concept of frontier offends us. In the year 1945 I visited in Paris a distinguished historian of philosophy, a Frenchman now deceased. I shall always recall with emotion his venerable appearance, to which the lack of one arm, lost in World War I, added a tragic note. His comments were brilliant—until the name of Heidegger came up in the conversation. At that point the old man almost flew into a rage. He referred to his "Bosch" colleague—that was his epithet—with utter contempt. Not on account of his teachings—these appeared to him to be taken essentially from Pascal, from Kierkegaard, and from Nietzsche—but because he had flirted with Nazism. Shall I hide the fact that this reaction profoundly pained me, just though it might have been? High culture is genuine to the degree that it transcends the mere peculiarity of nationalistic or group feelings and particularities in order to rise to the universal. On this level there ought to be no frontiers; and in fact we see that the finest spirits of Europe tend to transcend them, to consider themselves as representatives not of French, German, or Russian culture, but of European or Western culture.

Thus the cultural frontier is, strictly speaking, what separates and puts in opposition the masses who fall into our category called middle culture. These spiritual complexes are the ones whose description it is the main concern of an inquiry such as we have undertaken to effect; hence, I am going to use the term "cultural frontier" in this sense in the comparison we are now going to make between the two great American cultures that face one another on the frontier.

The Evaluation of Cultures

It seems to me that the scheme I have just suggested provides the only possible criterion for judging and ranking cultures and for explicating their fate in history. The quality of a culture depends on the degree of nobility or refinement in style of life that it represents, and this is clearly indicated by the degree to which universal values are present in it along with those of pure particularity.

It is well, then, not to lose sight of the distinction between the two. The values of particularity are those that are relative to the special tastes and preferences that result from a people's mode of existence, historical formation, and patterns of life. Hence they are not necessarily transferable to other human groups, though the latter may imitate them. On the other hand, the universal values are associated with the highest capacities proper to man as such, and therefore are models that embody what is desirable everywhere and always. The former are represented by customs and constitute the sole repertory of primitive peoples and the basic content of the others. Peoples are civilized in the degree to which universal values predominate and are effective in their lives.

These points of reference—particularity and universality—help us not only to place cultures on the level appropriate to each, but also to understand their character. Thus, for example, we have a clearer awareness of the sense in which we say that the barbarians were barbarous. We see why Greece embodied a kind of magisterial dignity for every age; and Rome, as one formed under this tutelage, occupied an intermediate position between "the miracle of Greece" and the rude primitivism that finally obliterated her frontiers. Furthermore, it becomes clear to us that this greater residual amount of primitivism is the reason why, despite the Greek superiority in universal values—or precisely because of it—Rome seems to us to have a less ideal personality, but a more energetic and vital one. The humanness of Greece attained such heights of purity and gentility that they virtually put her in a divine, Olympian category.

Pressed to give an example closer to home, I would venture to propose Spain and France. I believe no one will doubt that the latter is closer to having a system of universal values; the former, one more rooted in the particular and the concrete. When Unamuno called Paris, almost contemptuously, "that knowledge workshop," it is likely he was referring to the intellectual polarization that in France produces a uniform and comprehensive culture, not centered as that of Spain in the deeply rooted and primal. In Paris the novelist Camilo José Cela boasted to me about the mixture of Celtic and Carpeto-Vetonican* in him. Federico García Lorca liked to tell a story that illustrates what I want to suggest. A group of gypsies had gathered to hear the singing of a girl from their tribe whose voice they considered marvelous. Everyone applauded the performance except one very old gypsy who, on hearing the clear trills, uttered with muffled severity a single word of judgment: "Paris." The voice did not seem to him anything that belonged to his people, but to the Parisians. The young gypsy understood. She went to the back of the cave and downed a glass of whiskey. Then with scalded voice, she drew from her throat the hoarse pantings that the patriarch was missing—to which the latter responded with a kiss on her forehead.

This background of residual primitivism, inherent in the *personality* of a culture, or of its characteristic expressions, is what the Spanish call *solera* (base-stone). Its absence explains why peoples who are too young or have few traditions of their own always turn out to be a bit colorless or to have a purely adventitious particularity. Recognizing this, however, we must also admit that the degree to which universal values are present is the decisive matter in the cultural realm, since these values are the ones that clearly mark what is fundamentally human.

With this criterion we can also face the problem of evaluating indigenous cultures. By doing so we Latin Americans would avoid certain romantic contagions and political pressures that urge us to mourn over pre-Columbian ruins and remains. In order to admire the social organization and the engineering of the Inca we have to disregard too much their cost in slavery. So, too, is it necessary to remove from the mind the image of hearts trembling on the teocallis if we wish to appreciate with unadulterated sympathy what no doubt the Aztec calendar shows of the primitive mind's ingenious power in

---

*A mountain range in central Spain.—*Tr.*

the service of a characteristically human meaning: the sense of time. What deserves our continuing esteem in these cultures, apart from purely anthropological or archaeological interests, are the budding universal values—especially aesthetic values—that there were in them. But no indigenist piety should prevent us from observing that, in fact, those values were limited.

Nor is the criterion of which I speak valid only for judging remote cultures. Not many years ago we came to the point of bringing German culture to judgment because it seemed to fail us, and indeed officially failed, in regard to the conditions of universality and integrity. Then we had the painful impression that the great heritage of Goethe, of Kant, of Schiller and Hegel, suddenly was left submerged beneath a tremendous deficiency in human nobility, as a sacrifice of conscience and of sensibility on the bloody altars of national pride and political passion.

Finally, the same criterion is what today leads us, at least us of a certain spiritual makeup, to throw in our lot with the type of culture we call "Occidental." Occidentalism is not mere narcissistic regionalism, nor is it simple zeal for the survival of a particular system of political and social forms for their own sakes. As a synthesis of Greek rationalism, Christian spirituality, and Northern European voluntarism, the Occidental is, above all, the product of a very elaborate human discipline—one in which intelligence, moral and aesthetic sensibility, and creative energy freely interact, each limiting and compensating for the particular excesses of the others. This is why Western culture is naturally associated with the enjoyment of liberty and so resists those particularisms dominated by a single emphasis, which generally finds its social and political expression in authoritarian systems. It is especially important to note that Western values are not only, or even primarily, those associated with technological progress, as one tends to suppose. Technique is a mere process: a matter of methods and instruments. It can serve equally well the spiritual forms of life and refined brutality. Only an integral conception of values is able to orient it toward its most fruitfully human and universal application.

Let us observe, finally, that the values having this dimension of universality are also in essence perennial, and generally have little to do with mere current or circumstantial relevance. Many are impressed by a culture's superiority if it displays more modernity. Such a criterion is a residue of the old nineteenth century idea of automatic progress. Experience has now taught us that the new is not necessarily better and that, in the last analysis, the quality of a culture consists in the degree of nobility in the style of life it is able to produce; that is to say, in the degree to which it is able to satisfy the aptitudes and propensities that distinguish the human from the animal. It is a dimension of depth more than of breadth and is concerned more with the being of man than with his activity, his possessions, or his power.

The Destiny of Cultures

It is a bit disconcerting that, at first glance, the fortunes of history appear not always to have been responsive to this evaluation. Very refined cultures, such as those of ancient India and China, or that of classical Greece, succumbed beneath the impact of barbarian invasions or gave way to coarser styles of life. In the degree to which this is the case, it only demonstrates that even those cultures were imperfect. But the consideration of this phenomenon involves a limited historical perspective, whether in space or in time. The world of Lao Tse and Confucius, as well as that of the Brahman, by one means or another, withstood the disorders of history and even overran their original frontiers. The balkanized Greece of our times is a descendant of classical Greece, but those who received the inheritance of the latter were first Alexander and then the Christian world. In the worst cases, cultures disappeared as localized historical units; but what, if anything, they had of universal substance was passed on to enrich the larger circle of humanity.

Accordingly I do not put much credence in the decline of the West, with which Spengler alarmed us a few years ago. I do not know what the destiny of Europe as a *political* entity may be; but what is now evident is that she has gone on withstanding one crisis after another, and that come what may her culture is already widely extended in America, which continues to manage and enrich this living endowment with great vigor. No new power emerges in the world that does not begin by assimilating all it can from Europe. Sometimes it distorts her values and perverts her techniques with the remains of its special primitivism; but it is probable that such aberrations are only episodes in the broad sweep of time. If we were able to see the historical process in its widest perspective, we would discover, I believe, that it is a response, as it were, to the lure of universality, the complete affirmation of all those values that the great cultures have contributed to the ultimate destiny of men.

All of this brings us back to the frontier. When two cultures of very different intrinsic capabilities confront one another in a zone of conflict, history shows us that, in the end, the one with the most universal elements prevails, for the simple reason that it is the richest in capacities and resources. This is the explanation of the famous paradox—so marked in the classical example of Greece and Rome—that the culture of the vanquished sometimes absorbs that of the victors. This very thing occurred in the encounter of the Germanic peoples with those of the Roman tradition.

This absorption is not, however, a constant of history, as sometimes supposed. In the tremendous collision with the Indian on the American frontiers, in the North as well as in the South, the cultures of the vanquished disappeared as organic structures. This happened because, even in our continental areas, where those cultures were much richer and more closely knit, the particular almost entirely excluded the universal. Garcilaso the Inca wept as he recalled the traditions and customs of his maternal grandfathers, but in the end he went to Spain to be educated and became fascinated by Leo Hebraeus. It was not the so much overworked brutality of the conquest that imposed itself on the indigenous cultures, but rather—though at times our sentimental perspective does not let us see it—the intrinsic superiority of the Spanish culture, which in one way or another was reflected in the conquerors and the missionaries. They brought to America three important elements of universality: the Spanish language, richer in expressive resources than the indigenous tongues; Christianity, which placed in opposition to the various local primitive creeds a superior ethical and metaphysical conception, rooted in the solidarity of men and in supernatural transcendence in conduct; and the idea of law, whose norms were violated a thousand times in practice, but always acknowledged in spirit as superior to interest and mere custom.

Nevertheless, Spanish ecumenism allowed the traditions of the primitive cultures to subsist as the primitive base of Hispanic-American society, more or less catechized by the Hispanic. These Indian cultures communicated a considerable amount of their peculiarity to the creole* stratum, which thus came to be composed, as Martí would say, not of "grape Spaniards" but rather of "corn Spaniards" —people who prayed in churches with altars and porticos combining indigenous naturalism with peninsular baroque.

Meanwhile, another will to dominion was asserting itself in the North of the hemisphere, with a much less assimilative spirit, and moved by ethical and religious impulses as well as by economic and political ones. The clash of these two processes ended by fixing the cultural frontier at the Río Grande and the Antilles, and their respective development is one of the factors that characterize the two cultural masses that were thus left facing one another. The specifica-

---

*Whenever Mañach refers to the creole (Spanish *criollo*), he means those of Spanish descent born and raised in the American colonies of Spain.—*Tr.*

tion of these characteristics should tell us if there really is a possibility that the contact between them might be anything more than superficial and if it is worthwhile that it be so.

Two Psychologies

These cultures are defined by their respective middle levels. In the United States, the residual primitive elements—the Indian and the immediate progeny of the Spanish conquerors—and the newcomers—the Negro and the immigrants from continental Europe—lack importance in their effects on the general style of life. They represent, at the most, influences that are very marginal and oblique in certain regions. In Latin America, or at least in what exclusive of Haiti, we should call Hispanic, the indigenous and African elements have more deeply penetrated the culture of certain areas; but not to the extreme of essentially differentiating them from the creole pattern. As regards the respective intellectual minorities, they are also responsive to this dominant style, whether by consonance or dissonance.

The basic differential factor of both cultures is the bedrock of racial temperament. The current of collective experience subsequently acts upon it, but not without the modifications introduced to reflect that resistant substratum. In general, the historic process does no more than accentuate certain traits of the original character by particularly availing itself of them.

It is obvious that Americans of the North and of the South—let us speak of them thus for the sake of simplicity—have very different ways of feeling, of thinking, and of acting. As for ourselves, a certain friend of mine, the Chilean poet Barrenechea, likes to refer generously to our psychic community by saying that we Hispanics have the same "central heating." The metaphor is quite accurate, since temperature and temperament are related words, and all culture, as Américo Castro has said for his own purposes, is a "spiritual abode."

Another illustrious Spanish writer, Madariaga in his book *The English, the French, and the Spanish,* argued very persuasively, as many of you will recall, that the respective psychological keys to these founders of the American racial stock are will, reason, and intuition. As this latter is a special aptitude for grasping reality, or its requirements, without intellectual operations, we can consider it as one of the forms of sensibility. From all this it follows for the Spanish essayist that, in the field of conduct, what is proper and distinctive for the English is action; for the French, rational thought; for the Spanish, emotion.

This thesis, elaborated very ingeniously, is valid to the degree that such generalizations can be; that is to say, insofar as they rest upon what is most frequent or "typical." Moreover, it must be interpreted in reference to *accents* of temperament and of conduct; not to exclusive psychological modalities. The fact that Anglo-Saxons are mainly volitional does not prevent them from harboring sentimentalism, even though they may try to hide it. Neither does the predominence of sensibility in Hispanic people signify a purely emotional aptitude, but it may come to include, and in fact does include, a zest for the contemplation of ideas. At times their moral sensibility even serves as a drive for the most vigorous activity. What happens is that these other life styles are not the central ones, and thus are not the decisive ones for habitual conduct.

In conclusion, it would perhaps be more exact to say that the will of Anglo-Saxons tends to be calculating, and in that sense to be governed by reason; while the more improvising will of Hispanic people is directed by feeling. Consider the suggestiveness of the two meanings of our word *querer* [to want, to intend], affective and volitional. On the other hand, the English word "sensible" has nothing to do with our words *sensible* and *sensitivo*, but is synonymous with prudent, reasonable, and practical, values that the Anglo-Saxon holds in esteem comparable only to the care with which he conceals his own feelings. Emotion is likely to appear to him a disease, even though it be the sublime emotion of Othello. On the other hand, for people of our stock, what is imprudent is no obstacle to its being noble and glorious, as our master Don Quixote proved. And Martí—so much a "corn Spaniard"—gave the title of "the world's first-born" to the impassioned, that is, to people who are able to feel deeply.

There is an apparently unimportant social detail that very visibly marks this frontier between the two racial stocks. I refer to the form of greeting one another. Among Anglo-Saxons, even for two brothers who meet again after some time apart, it is sufficient to shake hands. Among Hispanic people, those who are only friends embrace profusely. I do not know if this greater effusiveness is due to our having a larger and more cordial affective capacity, or simply to our being more expressive in our gestures, like all the peoples living in the Mediterranean ambience or originating there. But I suspect that none of these explanations would suffice just by itself. In one of his recently published posthumous writings, Ortega y Gasset comments on what we might call the anthropology of the salutation. Shaking hands, he tells us, is a vestige of the way the primitive had of showing he was not carrying a weapon, and thus that he was not an enemy. It is too bad the Spanish philosopher did not pause also to consider the embrace. *A fortiori*, this would signify something more as a gesture of greeting. It would signify a desire for solidarity, for close association. I would even venture to suggest that these preferred modes of greeting represent two distinct types of individualism. That of the Anglo-Saxon always maintains a distance, perhaps so as to be better able to deploy judgment and action before committing oneself in a situation. That of the Mediterranean Latin, particularly that of the Spaniard, is a monopolizing, absorbing individualism, which tends to fuse everything into one's own self, to condition everything to one's own desire. We could almost say it is rather a kind of egotism.

Permit me another example whose commonplaceness lends itself to similar interpretations. In the United States, when one sees two men quarreling, one must be wary of intervening. I tried it several times in my younger years, and I always ran the danger of getting crucified. The Yankee "loves a good fight." He sees the fist fight as a manly struggle, a consumption of excess energy, and a way of adjudging the right of the stronger. This right demands that it be respected, even though it be in terms of every person being obliged to "mind his own business." In the United States, the foreigner is more foreign than anywhere else. Everyone goes his own way. The righting of wrongs is the business of the law and its agents, not of any private quixotism. In all of this there is, if you will, a substratum of brutality that probably is one of the residues of the frontier struggle. It represents a kind of cult of energy that, from this elementary plane of the fight, passing through fondness for the roughest sports, extends to those manifestations of competitive activity that go by the name of rugged individualism because of their resistance to the modifying action of the state.

Nevertheless, one must not forget the other ingredient, Puritanism, which as Santayana observed, also influences North American life in the broader form of a purely ethical dimension. This is the country where, once the distance between strangers has been overcome, friendship is wont to be firmer and more considerate, the spirit of social cooperation more generous, and the motivations of conduct reasonable and ingenuous sometimes to the point of frankness. This is the parallel in private life of the Puritan influence that I have already had occasion to note in reference to the nation's foreign relations.

If we again contrast this with the Latin psychology, we will note that the shift in individual conduct occurs now in the opposite direction. The generous expansiveness of the embrace is wont to give way to a personal reserve, a concentration on the self that it would hurt me to have to call egoism. It is rather that the heart is worn on the sleeve, and that actions and attitudes answer to its dictates, to the soul's *gana*. *Gana*—here is a word that is very much our own, one that has no adequate translation into any other language.* Count Keyserling observed that this experience, this kind of passive longing, is very characteristic of the South American; and you will recall that Ganivet said that the ideal of the Spaniard would be to be able to carry a certificate declaring him authorized to do whatever would satisfy his *gana*, or as we also say his *real gana*, his absolute *gana*.

Perhaps this helps to explain the different concepts or feelings that Anglo-Saxons and we Hispanic peoples have of liberty. In its golden centuries, Spain was docile about political absolutism with religious roots, as long as it respected the individual's personal jurisdiction. Until a very short time ago, anarchism was accepted as a tradition and even claimed the support of spirits of great nobility. All of this is inconceivable for the Anglo-Saxon. He sees liberty not as a principle or as an end in itself, but as something functional, a means for the development of his own capacities and for the effective use of his own energies, and he is not unaware of how much is contributed to this by having the whole social context infused with liberty and related values. We Hispanic peoples tend to be satisfied with its personal enjoyment. Martí, very much in the Spanish heritage, but more influenced by the United States than he himself realized, lamented that one of the "afflictions" of Latin American nations is having, as they do, the passion for liberty, they do not see how necessary the general welfare is in order to assure it.

Finally, I would like to give an example of our egocentrism that is of particular importance: our sense of dignity. I recall having read some time ago now an article by the North American essayist Edmund Wilson commenting on the art of Charlie Chaplin. He interpreted the pathetic humor of the great clown as an aspiration for dignity that was constantly frustrated by poverty and bad luck. According to Wilson, this frustration was never so concretely evident as when Charlie slipped on a banana peel and his little hat went flying grotesquely off to one side and his little cane to the other. Dignity was thus understood as something extrinsic: something to which one *aspired*. I believe I recall that Wilson—at the time much influenced by Marxism—concluded by suggesting that dignity consisted, at the most, of a mere social posture destined to disappear—a bourgeois excrescence.

---

*It is variously rendered as desire, appetite, inclination, longing, etc.—*Tr.*

Need I say how different all these extrinsic explications are from the concept we have of dignity? I am not referring to the long-standing philosophical concept that, since the Stoics, has associated it with the idea of the human person as an end in himself. Although ennobled by the Senecan tradition, dignity in Spain is something more than an ethical notion. It is a vital experience, an emotion, a central feature of character. It is not attributed to the person in abstract terms, but to the fully concrete individual: to the I. One does not *aspire* to it, one *has* it. It is not the heritage only of gentlemen, but even of beggars. Who has not noticed, even in the paintings of Velázquez, for example, that his fools, dwarfs, and buffoons show no less dignity than monarchs and courtiers? Dignity is one of the forms of gravity, not the physical gravity of Charlie Chaplin, but that which passes through the soul's axis. In other words, it is a way of feeling the weight of one's own person and of making others feel it. It is related to pride and to the keenest sense of honor, but less in a formal mode, and more as an essence, if I may express it thus. At times it produces a ridiculous self-love; but it is also capable of rising to heroic heights, the examples of which—often they are examples of sublime folly as well—abound in the history of all of our nations. In short, this dignity of ours has nothing to do with Charlie's spills. Don Quixote never shows his dignity more than when, beaten and battered, he reproaches the men of Yanguas from the ground.

Of course, Anglo-Saxons also have their dignity. A short time ago, I read in a North American magazine about the difficult situation in which the sporty photographer who married the sister of Britain's Queen Elizabeth found himself. Making a fine distinction, he said that his dignity as a consort did not permit him to engage in any occupation whatever; but on the other hand, his *self-respect* obliged him not to live without working. This comment almost undermined my thesis. But then I observed that the dignity and the self-respect he referred to clearly resulted from their dependence on something exterior. For us it is not so. Like *decoro*—another word very much our own*—dignity in the Spanish sense is a kind of predisposition, an end in itself, a necessary and sometimes sufficient condition for moral and social sensibility; in short, a sort of *a priori* of conduct.

I have lingered for some time on these psychological considerations, because I believe they are not irrelevant to the general theme of the frontier. These differences have a great deal to do with the problems of understanding between the two Americas. We all know how much concern these problems occasion today and how generally

---

*Circumspection, decency, civility—*Tr.*

ineffective have been the methods aimed at the improvement of the relations at issue. The usual recourse has been to economic expedients that, dictated in all good faith by the "practical sense" of the North, nonetheless collide with the noncalculable "dignity" of the South. Clearly it is almost always a matter of conflict of emphasis, or of mere forms. The North Americans cannot wish to injure us when they extend a hand to us, nor are we so excessively idealistic as to be blind to the utility of material resources. But no matter how sincere they may be, we do not like their simplistic view in which the implicit presumption seems to be that the only way to win our hearts is through material assistance. The question of forms—that is, of tact, of right occasion, and of formulation—is fundamental in dealing with people who wear their dignity on their sleeve. We are molded in the tradition of that noble character Lazarillo de Tormes who, at the usual time for digesting a meal, concealed his hunger by a toothpick in his mouth.

In short, the difficulty of finding a point of tangency between the two circles of value, centered respectively in will and sensibility, in doing and being, suggests with respect to our inter-American relations, the degree to which the diplomacy that is employed in dealing with them might profitably be shaped by the insights of comparative psychology. Hence our cultural frontier, and your Puerto Rican frontier particularly, could be a good school. It appears that it is going to be just that.

Two Historical Processes

All that I have set forth about the psychology of the Anglo-Saxon and the Hispanic peoples involves the implicit premise that we American offshoots of these founding peoples do not differ markedly from them. In fact, assuming that he is truly "typical," any North American behaves like an Anglo-Saxon, and no moderately representative Latin American of Spanish descent fails to harbor the Spaniard within, though he may sometimes deny it. What blood does not do the culture does. Even the children of immigrants with other origins end up appearing as though they were formed in those primal spiritual molds. To me it did not seem odd, but instead rather accidentally profound, that at a political meeting in Cuba a black orator should say very naturally: "Because we Latins . . ."

Nevertheless, it cannot be doubted that, on this side of the Atlantic, the different circumstances—the physical and social environment, racial crossbreeding, immigration, and above all, accumulated collective experience—have introduced modifications in the original character, whether they be, as I have already said, by way of smoothing off certain edges or strengthening such and such features. The magnitude and openness of the American environment favor freedom of movement and, in the social sphere, suppression of hierarchies. Mixture with the Indian and with the black generates biases and tensions, but also stimulates the rooting of worth in the purely human, and not in the formalities of caste or social position. The immigrant stream, which has been so powerful in some of our countries, forces the assignment of merit in terms of accomplishment, and has not failed to open American societies to certain cosmopolitan influences.

But it is above all the historical process that has continued to substantially modify both the English culture inherited by the North and the Spanish culture we received from Spain. In the last lecture I very briefly referred to this process from the political viewpoint and in relation to the final determination of our frontier. Now it would be helpful to see it in cultural perspective. Incidentally, a comparison of the two lines of development will also allow us to understand better why, in so many respects, Latin America—let us say it without dissimulation—is backward as measured against North America, in spite of there being between them a certain commonality of drives and of historical calling.

The comparison can be reduced to a few contrasts. The English penetration of America was initially a *private* undertaking: the work of religious and even political dissidents. The Puritans of New England, like the Quakers later, drew their spiritual and social discipline from themselves. They provided their own authority, their own church, their own code. Thus the Anglo-American was born beneath the sign of ideological and moral autonomy. To the South, on the other hand, the New World undertaking was carried out under the auspices and vigilance of the crown and the Catholic church, and generally was subjected to the administrative discipline of these powers, with more or less compliance by the conquerors. From their beginning, the life of the Spanish colonies bore the seal of authority.

Initially the colonization of the North was very localized and very slow in expanding. It was more a question of refugees on the defensive than of conquerors. Not until well along in the sixteenth century did the first settlements adopt a dynamic of conquest, moved by pressures that were mainly economic. The expansion then was the work of a number of separate nuclei in a lively competition of initiatives and efforts. It was quite the opposite in the South, where the drive for conquest appeared from the start, led by powerful individuals who were moved by the crusading spirit as much as by the ambition for wealth. This drive, already exhausted in the sixteenth century, was transformed by the fears of the crown itself into a rigid colonial organization, based on large administrative zones with little intercommunication and very strict control from the mother country. Thus while the colonial reality of the North, at first dispersed, progressed toward unity in a common effort to extend the frontier, that of the South, initially united at least in its spirit, declined toward formal plurality. This was already the germ of the future "Disunited States of America."

Notwithstanding their character as religious minorities, the Mayflower Pilgrims and the other expatriots carried to America, stimulated by freedom of belief, the critical and inventive spirit of the then emerging English bourgeoisie, which three centuries later was to be the driving force of the industrial revolution. Thus it was that their initial quietism as refugees in the end gave way to an economic activism, the first natural objective of which was to enlarge their territory. This expansion proved to be relatively easy, in a terrain that was not generally very rugged and in the face of scattered nuclei of natives without any political or cultural cohesion. Nor were they troubled by scruples. The narrow ethical sense of Puritanism, deeply rooted in particularist attitudes of a communitarian nature, messianic and even racial, was not embarrassed by decimating the Indian in order to occupy his lands.

In the South the spirit transmitted to the colonial arena was that of the Counter Reformation: militantly religious, eager to compensate for the territory Catholicism had lost in Europe, and suspicious of outside intrusions and naturalism. The Spaniards catechized the Indians, though they were confronted with relatively mature and resistant indigenous cultures and had to operate in extraordinarily variable terrain. This explains why the frontiers of expansion and conquest contracted, becoming transformed into the purely defensive boundaries of the early established political units. In fact, beginning with the sixteenth century the colonies lived with their backs to these frontiers, feeding off of their own substance. The zest for the activity of domination atrophied into a sort of formalism and internal social parasitism based on the labor of Indians, blacks, and mestizos. Instead of the leveling and liberating influence of the frontier, our colonies suffered a profound deformation of hierarchies.

Also separation from the mother country proved to be much easier for the British offspring. Free from any possible indigenous adulteration, the ties of blood and language that united them to England proved not to be affected by independence, which from the beginning had been fostered by virtual political autonomy and the precedents of English political thought itself starting with Locke. It was enough, then, that when the economic exactions of the crown became sufficiently onerous, subjection to it became untenable. The relatively easy communication among the thirteen colonial units expedited their mutual understanding.

In the South, by contrast, the colonial subjection, already well supported by the lack of communication among vice-royalties and captaincies and by a much more compact organization of the mother country's power in each of them, was also rooted in feelings of loyalty and solidarity with Spain, which the presence of large indigenous masses in the bosom of those societies helped to accentuate, and which, besides, were only slowly undermined by liberal ideas. It was necessary that the basis of political solidarity break down, through Spain's being left without a head as a result of the Napoleonic invasion, in order for the colonies in question to be concerned with a destiny of their own. Under these circumstances, the process of separation witnessed a division among the creoles themselves, and had the character of a civil war much more definitely than that of the North.

Independence united the North Americans still further, leaving them with the limited political problem of the federal organization of the states, with their reservations of sovereignty, within a broad framework of democratic solidarity that was threatened only by slavery. The immediate historic task consisted in pushing forward the frontier. In this undertaking the northeastern and central states chiefly collaborated, with those of the slaveholding South remaining only on the margin of it, and thus more disconnected from the national interest.

By contrast, from Mexico to the Río de la Plata, the greater physical and administrative separation of colonial units extending over much vaster areas caused the impulse to emancipation to arise in different centers. Even in those places that at the beginning presented a front of cooperation, as in South America, it was not long before fragmentation occurred. The will to nationhood crystallized prematurely, limiting itself to the more or less contentious delimitation of the respective territories. Within each of the republics thus created—principally by the work of strong individuals who were more gifted than prudent—the weakness of cohesion forced into the focus of attention the rivalry between conservatives and liberals, between centralizers and federalists, between constitutionalists and political chiefs. In our countries political passion was the order of the day, as it was at the time in Spain, whose blood we inherited. Attention to social and economic problems had to wait almost a century until, in the Disunited States of our America, the countless internal convulsions might be resolved by more or less effective constitutional means.

In the North, with the frontier carried to the Pacific, the Indian decimated, subjected, and rendered marginal, the new republic could apply itself to new tasks: "rounding out" its territory and overcoming the crisis of slavery in order to give the nation the political and moral unity it still lacked. Following the first expansive movements at the expense of Spain, France, and Mexico, came the only internal convulsion the country has known: the War of Secession. The triumph of abolitionism also cleared the way for economic consolidation through the balancing of industry and agriculture and the unification of the internal market. English immigration was virtually at a standstill after Independence. This and subsequent conflicts with England meant that her traditions promptly ceased to influence North American life. The process of nationalization began there much before it did among us. On the other hand, without human resources proportionate to its enormous territorial scope and with the necessities of economic development, the United States had to open itself to large-scale immigration, principally European. This in turn made necessary an intensive campaign of attraction and assimilation. The image of "the land of opportunity" was cultivated, in which no prejudice would prevent the immigrant from enjoying all his rights, and where a vigorous impetus was given to public education in order to unify the civic consciousness. Thus began the process of crowning political democracy with social democracy, free from particularist traditions and rigid hierarchies. The famous "melting pot" produced a new, essentially cosmopolitan national substance, and a style of thought and life more than ever open to the new. However, this could not be achieved without inevitable tensions in the religious sphere, in close personal relations, and in the culture. It may be said that only in our time has the United States arrived at national integration.

In Latin America, with regard to such matters, the circumstances were different. Crossbreeding with the Indian began from the start. Once the war of independence and its most immediate consequences were finished with, Spanish blood began to flow again toward the former colonies. Traditionalism held its own in customs, being partially challenged only in the spheres of political ideas and letters. In spite of the slogan of "educating the ruler," public education advanced very slowly. The republics that had been seats of viceroyalties maintained their colonial style, and it is significant that only the others, with a more open social texture, like those of the Río de la Plata area, opened themselves to immigration of non-Spanish origin. However, even there the cohesion of the creole mass absorbed the alien stream, incorporating it into the Hispanic tradition. In short, Latin American society, in spite of its mestizo variation, has up to our own days kept itself more faithful than the North to the original mold.

The year 1898, stained with the blood of two peoples, marked for the United States that initial point of maturity in which a nation, with its internal organization and establishment already consummated, could begin to allow itself the luxury of exterior commercial and political adventures. That year is a decisive one in more than one sense. It drew the United States out of its isolation, out of its position of being purely receptive and cordial in relation to the things of Europe, initiating it into the stage of responsibilities that would lead it to its present international preëminence. It provoked Spain into a total inward withdrawal that found its cultural expression in the Generation of '98 and in the larger constellation of efforts that Aubrey Bell has called the birth of modern Spain. For our America the year 1898 completed the political separation from our historical matrix, giving birth to those new offspring of uncertain viability, Cuba and Puerto Rico, and presenting to us with new urgency the general problem of the frontier.

But what I want to emphasize now, in conclusion, is that throughout the long process of which that year was the culmination, the United States continued to benefit from the advantage of having become independent almost a half century before our Southern republics did. This fact by itself ought to weigh more heavily than it usually does in the customary outlook when one speaks of the "backwardness" of Latin America in comparison to North America. But it is well to note how many other causes of an internal character, not always under our control, contributed to creating a more complex situation than that in the North and to explaining this lack of synchronization.

Reducing this comparison to its simplest formulation, we could say that in the United States the process has been open, rapid, and innovative; ours has been closed, slow-moving, conservative. There, it was continually nourished with fresh contents; here, because of a profound loyalty to tradition, which independence was unable to diminish, we preferred to season the old contents with the new. Historical experience obliged the North American to transcend himself, by mobilizing above all the springs of will and of action. The Spanish American, instead, was led to turn inward, finding his stimulus in sensibility, always close in these lands of ours to that boiling point that we call passion. All that they possessed by way of calculation with a view to action we possessed in the form of spontaneity and even ingenuousness, in defense of our own being.

From this follows a difference in the modulation of cultural patterns transmitted by the respective founding nations. But the consideration of this matter calls for some careful scrutiny and thus the further benefit of your generous attention. Let us then leave it for the next lecture.

IV

The American

Cultural Frontier

At the end of the last lecture we were saying that the historical process in the Americas produced different modifications in the two great cultures of America with respect to their original patterns, that of the English and the Spanish. Now we are going to try to make these differences more precise in order to advance our understanding of the contrast between the two cultural masses that face one another on the frontier.

A Culture of Action

In the last lecture, we saw that, in its broadest sense, the word culture covers the normal temper of life and spirit of a people. Thus, the culture of England appears to be characterized by a kind of duality, by a certain tendency to be deployed between the intrinsic and the extrinsic, between sensibility and will, between reflection and action. More conventionally, we might also say that England's culture is deployed between idealism and realism. Of course these two poles are found in all advanced cultures. But some, like that of Spain, tend to integrate the values corresponding to them; in others, like that of England, these values operate disjunctively—the religious, the ethical, and the aesthetic are separated from the convenient and practical. Politics is then a sort of intermediate zone, leaning sometimes toward one pole, sometimes toward the other, but which, simply by virtue of its character as action, tends more toward realism than toward idealism.

History, and perhaps geography, has much to do with this polarity. England, master of her destiny at least since the twelfth century, early developed habits and attitudes of the kind we might call centripetal: a conservative and traditionalist spirit that has never ceased being its outstanding feature; a concern for hierarchies and forms; an individualism jealous of personal freedom and independent judgment, insistent on consent as the condition of political power. But then, whether because of the combativeness natural to islands, as Ganivet thought, or because of political and economic necessities, by the Elizabethan period England felt imperial urges. For her, this centrifugal projection was a bit like what the frontier was to be for her American offspring. She put the values of reflection and sensibility alongside the values of expansive action. Aggressiveness, zest for profitable risk, the calculations of practical reason were superimposed on all overt behavior. The irritation implicit in the epithet "perfidious Albion" stems basically from this duality, which in the Victorian period was not exempt from certain forms of subtle hypocrisy.

Well then, this duality was transmitted to America. Favored here by new circumstances, it became the deep root of the other duality, which Santayana pointed out, between Puritanism and the frontier spirit. While the need for active expansion lasted, the frontier spirit prevailed, and it still in large part provides the characteristic accent of North American life, the basis of which was not the indigenous Indian cultures, which have hardly left a trace, but the pioneer force that subdued them. But already by the second half of the last century the abolitionist movement began to witness a reaction of the underlying ethical consciousness. The need for unity that the Civil War left in its wake was reinforced by the stream of immigration. This broadening of the spirit of human integration at the expense of racial, ideological, and political exclusivism helped to ripen the democratic sentiment and gave rise at length to a mixture of idealism and realism that frequently puzzles superficial observers.

The culture of the United States is impregnated with this dual spirit, which does not always succeed in integrating itself. In the last analysis, almost all its negative aspects are harmful aftereffects of the frontier, beginning with the virtually complete orientation of life toward economic values. This has resulted in a preoccupation with utility, which culminates in babbittry, with its scorn of purely intellectual and aesthetic values and a predilection for quantifiable and mass values, with the inevitable standardization thus generated. North Americans seem to crave the superlative and the new simply because they are so. Their frenetic haste accentuates the competitive tension of daily life.

The frontier experience is perhaps to blame for a certain biological arrogance, which may be the basis for racial discrimination and the lack of decisiveness in overcoming so grave a problem. The devaluing of humanism and of general education in the universities can also be attributed to the frontier outlook. Finally, the simple-mindedness of popular taste, which causes the United States to be represented so largely by the images of Hollywood and newspaper comic strips, may well be one more way of avoiding the sense of spiritual emptiness that the most frank of the country's writers persistently see behind the brilliant façade of North American life.

But let us not forget that many of the most positive aspects of that life are also a consequence of the original frontier spirit, and that these are now universal values within a particular context. An example is the innovating and experimental dynamism of pragmatic thought, so unjustly disdained by European academic philosophies. Another is the enormous contribution of the United States to scientific and technical advance. Others are the elaboration of an effective democratic system, despite certain internal failures such as that of ethnic discrimination, to which I have just referred; the exaltation of work as a source of human dignity; and that optimism and confidence in progress that North America offers as opposition to the defeatism and anxiety that threaten Western culture.

We should also not forget that North America's sense of life is not always that of something exclusively economic, nor is its cult of "success" purely a matter of gain. I have heard an anecdote about Edison that is very significant in this regard. The great inventor became associated with an entrepreneur and between them they spent a considerable sum on a certain industrial project that turned out not to be viable. The day they arrived at that conclusion Edison said to his associate, "But we had a good time trying, didn't we?" This zest for effort and for exploration, this capacity for assuming risks, this determined will to oppose inertia and routine, form part of the general cult of energy that is the mainspring of the American soul, and without doubt, the most essential legacy of the frontier.

When this spirit is combined with the idealistic impulse, the result is, I repeat, an ethical-practical synthesis manifesting itself in the surprising consideration of certain customs, in the self-critical mentality, often humble and always respectful of the merit of others, and in the active disposition to be generous with one's own wealth. This modulation is, finally, the basic reason why the United States, after giving free rein to the will to empire in its first historical stage, visibly checked it, then participated in two great world wars without seeking further advantage, and threw in for good measure economic assistance to many countries, including those that were enemies. Finally, the United States has become the guardian of political liberty to such an extent that, without it, who knows what fate would have befallen democracy in the world.

A Culture of Sensibility

Faced with the Anglo-Saxon culture thus modulated in North America, what is the profile of the culture stemming from the Hispanic tradition in our family of nations?

If the formula were not perilously mechanical, we would say that the emphases are inverted for better and for worse. But note that I say *emphases:* that is, not the values themselves, but the relative rank we ascribe to them. In the North, as we have just seen, the highest points on the scale of preferences are those that depend mainly on the will. In the South, the preferences are those that flow from the sensibility, in the broad sense in which I have been using the word, so as to include not just aesthetic sensitivity but also ethical sensitivity, that of the conscience, and the contemplation of ideas as objects of interest in themselves, without reference to their practical value. Precisely this sort of moral and intellectual aestheticism is one of the modulations that the America called Latin has superimposed on the Spanish legacy.

The core of the peninsular soul was formed in the battle of the Reconquest, which naturally brought with it an interpenetration of the religious and the political. Once the nation was constituted, the realistic demands of daily life had to be disciplined according to the ideal principles that had animated that historic effort for eight centuries. Even in letters there is testimony to this integration. The realist-idealist duality, which in the fifteenth-century *Celestina* we still see severed into opposite poles, is overcome in the aesthetic humanism of the Renaissance. By way of the picaresque on one side and the mystical on the other, this duality ends up in the synthesis of *Don Quixote* and the theater of the Golden Age.

This same duality, already on the way to integration, was brought to America by the conquistadors and the missionaries; but the physical and social setting of the New World tended to frustrate a unification similar to that of the peninsula. With the passing of the initial moments of the conquest, the vastness of the territory and its distance from Spain caused the relaxing of the cohesion of interests that action had imposed. In the regions where the creole had to continue fighting the Indian for many years, as happened in Chile, the social tone was more energetic and dynamic. This has been reflected in greater political integration, in a certain sobriety in customs, and in a tendency in letters toward the historical and didactic more than toward the humanistic and poetic. Recall the famous polemic between Andrés Bello and Sarmiento.* On the other hand, the vice-

---

*Mañach here refers to a prot' acted debate that took place during the mid-nineteenth century between Bello, a Venezuelan grammarian, and Domingo Faustino Sarmiento, an Argentine polemicist, over traditional and free literary styles.—*Tr.*

royalties, which assimilated the Indian, though only at an inferior social level, developed a genteel, ornamental culture imitative of peninsular formalism. This did not prevent the precipitating out at its base the melancholy of the subject race, whose predominantly aesthetic sensibility manifested itself in the popular arts, the forms of which were obliquely grafted on to baroque porticos and altars. By this double route, then, the culture of almost all of our America came to be impregnated with formalism.

Nevertheless, little by little the creole mass was producing a cultured minority in the highest sense of the word—eager for historical foundations and for more universal ideas. Dazzled since the second half of the eighteenth century by the distant glow of the Enlightenment that Charles III had allowed to penetrate the peninsula itself, this minority promoted the awakening from the famous "colonial slumber." The great news first of the North American revolution and then of the French sharpened the critical sense. Impatience about the future was superimposed on the long-established authority of the state, encrusted with tradition and routine. The decadent Scholasticism was felt as an obstacle. Into the consciousness of the educated creoles a new idea began vaguely to insinuate itself—the idea that America, all America, was the land promised to human hope by the Renaissance utopias. All of this provided the spiritual germ of independence.

The struggle for emancipation left in its wake societies characterized by the conflict between the old loyalties and the new "liberal" spirit. The social climate became more open and more dynamic. The old hierarchies were laid low, overwhelmed by the leveling tendency inherent in democratic impulses. On the battlefield the rural creole and the urban mestizos and blacks acquired rights. Like Napoleon's soldiers, many of the former carried in their knapsack the marshal's insignia and became political chieftains. This expansion of human possibilities set the tone of the new republics. The individual came to be less centered in himself, more ready for polemics, but also for fellowship and sympathy in the moral connotation of the word. Dignity was no longer a matter of race or of caste but a characteristic of every person.

In the subsequent formative period, political passion absorbed all the energies of society. Rebellion took precedence over authority and discipline, and in the absence of the traditional supports itself generated the public power. Few outside restraints were able to moderate it. The hierarchies had remained attached to the old order. The education of the public did not yet have an effective social dimension. The instinctive impulses had primacy. Even religiosity was in crisis. It was giving way in the educated classes to an incipient naturalism; for the rest it now lacked that urgent, almost dramatic, meaning that it was wont to have in Spain. In the most cultivated minority, the ethical sensibility of the race was overlaid by a political and aesthetic sensibility. One can say that in literary matters America was romantic. With the Scholastic tradition swept away and the classical tradition very much on the defensive, the vacuum left by them was promptly filled by the new feeling for American images, so much nurtured in Europe itself. Later appeared the positivist surge without its being able to overcome the distaste for the scientific; but our higher culture broadened itself with curiosities and cosmopolitan elements that served as a sieve for the romantic material. From all of this was constructed in large part the modernist movement through which our literature for the first time moved ahead of that of Spain.

Unquestionably the passage of more than a half century since that time has brought about many innovations in the general life style of Latin America. It could not be otherwise, open as these young societies are to influences and attractions whose routes of access have been constantly enlarging. On the other hand, one of their characteristics has come to be precisely the temptation to subordinate tradition to calling, reverence for the past to impatience about the future. Nevertheless, in its foundations—and the foundations are always what count most in making a characterization—our culture continues to be more subjective and more centered in the person and in sensibility than that of the North.

If we wanted to have a more concrete representation of this comparison, we could find it in the different designs customarily manifested in the respective centers of population. The basic scheme of a typical small city in the United States consists of a few parallel main streets that shoot straight out as if headed eagerly for a distant frontier. This is the pattern of archetypal Gopher Prairie in *Main Street*, the famous novel by Sinclair Lewis. By contrast, the Latin American city has as its kernel a central plaza with a church, and surrounding it a more or less haphazard maze of streets and alleys. Our cities are "modernized" to the degree that new forms of life obligate them to supplement this pattern with that of the United States; but we all feel that what is characteristically ours is the old urban core.

This centering of our towns and cities on a living core also represents the nuclear idea of our culture, despite the additions of modernity. Ours is a centripetal culture, rooted in genuine intimacy, a culture of satisfactions more than of efforts, and of motives and tastes more than of ends. It is responsive to the concept of life not as an enterprise, as an occasion for action, but as an end in itself, an opportunity to *be*. We expect from the life of each day what North Americans reserve for the time when they are retired from business. I believe that this gives us a capacity for enjoyment that in general makes us happier. But this does not necessarily mean greater frivolity on our part. Life for us is a spectacle to watch at the same time we enjoy our role as actors—passionate actors. We are not, therefore, incapable of action, but the acts and the accomplishments that we prefer are those that move our souls. A beautiful custom, the personality of a public figure, or frequently, a landscape or a splendid manifestation of nobility, tend to interest a genuine Latin American more intensely than a business transaction, a factory, or a new invention.

Of course the values that such preferences imply are sometimes universal, though the preferences themselves may have a particular character. The beauty of a work of art is no less universal than the explanatory formula of a scientific problem, because the enjoyment of the one and the discovery of the other presuppose the activity of the most noble and most characteristic functions of the human spirit. Besides the outstanding contributions that the high culture of Latin America has already made in the fields of literature and art, from Sor Juana Inés and Alarcón to Darío and Vallejo, I think it is right to point out that our social qualities of great human value often pass unnoticed and without sufficient appreciation. Excessively centered in the person, our culture is, by the same token, prodigal in those exemplary affirmations of personality that enrich the human scene. On the highest levels, these personalities throughout history have shown themselves capable of discharging their passion and their thought into heroic action out of which nations have sprung. Imbued with sympathy in the most profound sense of the word, the Latin American soul feels as few others do the dignity of the human. Our race relations, for example, demonstrate an uncoerced integration that today more than ever can serve as an example to the world. In the social and political realm, our peoples are eager for justice and freedom and there are few who have shed so much blood on their behalf. If particular interests at times excessively agitate or anger us in these spheres of public action, our common life proves to be free of the frenzy, the harshness, and the anguish that afflict other civilizations.

As for the rest, we need not disguise our limitations. Like the culture of the North, ours has deficiencies and excesses that correspond to its most effective resources. The egoistic aspect of our individualism tends to ascribe values to the person to the detriment of the collectivity. From this comes the somewhat anarchic passion for freedom, to which I have already made reference, and other political vices such as bossism, the cult of personality, and sectarian partisanship. The excessive subordination of ends to abstract principles translates itself into a concern with the present shortsighted about the future and into a disdain for external reality that serves idle theorizing more than practical sense. Our inclination to be abstract may well protect us—though not so much as we boast—from excessively valuing material goods, but it also hinders us from sharing that "sense of reverence for money" that the Spanish journalist Ramiro de Maeztu never ceased to admire in Anglo-Saxons as their stimulus for creative economic activity.

Even a spirit as little inclined as that of Martí to negative judgments deplored—in one of his least disseminated works, to be sure— these faults of the Latin American. Our people have a passion for freedom, he said, but they feel it as a right more than as a duty; as a personal dimension or desideratum, and not as a means for the realization of the general welfare, which is the condition for the preservation of personal freedom itself. And as for the other extreme, to which I have referred, he added that in our America "the force of passion" has tended to be "greater than the force of interest: Money is despised; the idea is worshipped." He concluded by saying that what presaged better times for these republics was that such contrary impulses were beginning to balance themselves out, "which would be beneficial for some time, in order to compensate with the temporary excess of one force for what is permanently present in the other." For our part we must recognize that this forecast is being fulfilled and that we no longer have as much of a basis as we once did for chiding North Americans for their materialism.

Our high, or minority, culture is rather detached from the middle level in which such traits present themselves, but nevertheless has profound affinity for it. To the pragmatism of the North, it put in opposition an overemphasis on theoretical judgments and aesthetic tastes. Our universities generally continue to be too concerned with rhetoric and with routinely issuing diplomas. Among us literature and art reveal more refinement of sensibility than creative or critical energy. Finally, only the youthfulness of our countries can excuse this high culture for what now is long-standing in Spain. It has not to any appreciable extent made progress in the natural sciences and technology. In this domain it is a parasitic culture.

A few years ago Giovanni Papini really irritated us Latin Americans with the reproach that we had not contributed anything substantial to the great tasks of the world. We might say—recalling

Unamuno's distinction—that the Italian writer was less wanting in truth than in fairness. We have already seen how our historical development obliged us to invest our best energies in remaking ourselves from an obstinate tradition to the calling that the new age had awakened in us. It is true that we had the advantage of being potential heirs of the example and the fruits of the four great modern historical mutations: the Renaissance and the Reformation, the democratic revolution and the industrial revolution. But this in turn presupposed that we had to assimilate at one stroke everything that Western culture had developed over four centuries, and all our special physical, demographic, social, and economic circumstances stood in the way of the rapidity of this absorption. If they had not seen themselves called above all to take care of immediate needs, what might not have been contributed, in the realm of "pure," timeless, universal creation, by men like Bolívar and Bello, like Sarmiento and Alberdi, like Juárez and Justo Sierra, like Montalvo and Hostos, like Martí and Varona, and many, many other talented ones, who wore themselves out in the generous task of freeing and organizing our nations, of educating them and driving them forward?

However, I am not going to commit the error I was deploring at the close of my last lecture, that of ducking responsibilities. When we have accounted for all the extenuating circumstances, it will still remain incontestably true that we are backward in all that part of the historical task that pertains not to sensibility but to the other faculties of the spirit. In order to liquidate this deficit we must reorient our own energies better and make ourselves fruitful by the emulation of others' examples.

I said earlier that if there is any criterion for such an evaluation, it will have to rest on the sum of universal values that each culture possesses, understanding by these the ones that to the highest degree fulfill the aptitudes and aspirations of man as a being with reason, sensibility, and conscience. It is precisely this triple dimension of the human spirit that makes it so difficult to order cultures hierarchically, since it happens that even those of the highest pedigree are slanted with each one in favor of its preferred type of values. On the other hand, the estimation of the others is generally subject to oscillations determined by changes in the general world situation and even at times by certain swings in standards of historical judgment.

Since at least the eighteenth century, and more markedly since the decline of romanticism and the apogee of positivism, the value of reason has been on the rise. In large part this is the cause of the prestige of what we call Western culture, for though it has always been characterized by its integrity, there is no doubt that the faustian values have been preëminent. Since these rational values are precisely those that have been most accentuated in Anglo-Saxon culture—which moreover has understood how to exploit them to the utmost in their technical application, giving them an enormous popular reputation for usefulness—it is natural that that culture should have called the tune in the world for more than half a century.

However, in our times this predominance has brought about a crisis. The experience of two wars and the whole social situation that they engendered have caused many reflective spirits to think about the insufficiency of a scientific and technical knowledge that has not succeeded in orienting the world toward the establishment of peace, security, and freedom. Every day one hears more talk of the crisis of the West, and many venture the belief that the contemporary malady would be remedied if there were greater hospitality to the spiritual values of Oriental culture, which in the last analysis are those of sensibility and awareness. What the man of today needs—it is said—is a return to the soul, to spirituality. With an opinion even closer to our own, has one not also heard it said, and by no one less than a Karl Vossler, that Spain—the old Spain with her proverbial "decadence"—is "the world's moral reserve"? Has not Ganivet's thesis about Spain's "virginity" been revived, coming paradoxically to signify her ability to contribute to the creation of a more humane and generous epoch?

I must say that, flattering though such pronouncements are, I do not believe it is wise to subscribe in any absolute way to the remedies they propose. Though this criticism still functions on a philosophical plane, there are already more than enough indications that under prevailing cultural circumstances the primacy of reason is giving way before an increasingly dangerous wave of pure irrationalism and blind vitalism. Huizinga, Russell, Sorokin, Massis, and many more have felt impelled in the face of the new romantics to denounce the lack of intellectual, moral, or aesthetic responsibility apparent in certain expressions of our time, from manners to philosophy, politics, and art. The pendulum has swung to the other extreme.

To remain fixed in that position would also mean a distortion of the human, another way of surrendering to pure spontaneity, so fertile in every sort of improvisation and arbitrariness. If it is true that under the cloak of practicality, of being scientific, of being efficient, not a little violence has been inflicted on the moral order, it is no less true that so-called idealism, or the bigotry that frequently hides behind the invocation of spiritual values, also does not have a conscience free of hypocrisies and abdications.

Although the conclusion may be very conventional and trite, it continues to be true that the most certain hope for human improvement resides in the old Greek watchword of harmony. Reason and sensibility are mutually complementary functions, in whose integration the highest in man is achieved. If the former analyzes the structures and processes of reality, the moral and aesthetic sensibility is what values that reality and suggests the ways of opening up channels into it toward the optimum human destiny; it is conscience that dictates, for example, that the latest nuclear science must serve the good of humanity and not its destruction. The Rilkes and the Tagores will always be no less necessary than the Einsteins and Edisons. Exclusive emphasis in favor of any of these dimensions of the spirit to the detriment of the rest represents only passing historical preference. The great human task for the future is to learn how to direct history by means of culture; to save history from brief reactions, and even more from the blind mechanism of rhythmic cycles; to achieve, finally, ever higher and more profound syntheses between the theses and the antitheses that constantly try to enslave it.

The Possible Synthesis

Judged by this criterion the Anglo-Saxon and the Latin cultures, that which the United States inherited and that which is the patrimony of our America, have no reason to exclude one another, but on the contrary they are called to complement and enrich one another.

Surely, that of the North is more penetrated than is ours with a preference for the rational and concrete. It is, as we have already seen, a culture centered in technique: in effective control over men and things. But it would be unjust to maintain that this emphasis excludes other values. On this level, the great Rodó from his empyrean will forgive us for no longer being able to subscribe to his judgment, according to which our America would be the heavenly realm of Ariel, and the North the den of Caliban. Such a judgment may well have served to contain our fits of positivist enthusiasm at the beginning of the century; but since then, experience has made us more cautious and knowledge, more just. Now we know that even in the field of middle culture, not only are seeds of thought also planted in the North, but that they are generously fertilized so as to yield the most abundant harvest. And in regard to the high culture of our neighbors, it would be plain ignorance not to recognize the fecundity with which for at least half a century it has been contributing to scientific research and artistic creation on the highest levels of universality. It is precisely that minority of writers, of educators, of scientists who, with the greatest clarity, indict the excesses of the middle

culture of their nation—the babbittry, the standardization, the super-
ficiality, the provincial self-satisfaction, the cult of the machine and
gadget, Hollywood and the comics.

On the other hand, we tend to take refuge in the advocacy of
what we have, perhaps as a defense mechanism or as a disguise for I
don't know what inferiority complex. Without any doubt our limitations are real. We have unilaterally put, and still are accustomed to
put, the emphasis on sensibility and on our particular forms of consciousness, which are not always of universal dimension. Other limitations are only historical. Our culture in general is less up-to-date,
less attuned to the concrete and material needs of today's world. But
this is far from signifying that we are contributing nothing to the
human scene.

Along with our insufficiencies in rationality and efficiency, at
the same time we show a certain breadth and depth in feeling and in
embodying the human, which is manifested, for example, in our
spontaneous forms of racial coexistence and in our greater propen-
sity for quality than for quantity, for the refinements of being than
for the achievements of power or possession. Finally, we show a
greater infusion of the soul in our behavior, which many today see
as the only hope for the world. To a life of the West that too much
tends to become anxious and frenetic, we still offer our certain joy-
ous confidence and serenity. It may be that we still carry the Mediterranean in our blood, which opposes the more combative Nordic
vitality.

But let us not deceive ourselves: These are no more than emphases, dependent on historical conditions. The firmest truth it
seems permissible to assert is that in both cultures, that of the North
and that of the South, along with distinctive traits, universal values
are manifest, or more precisely, elements capable of contributing to
a genuinely human culture by virtue of their universal appeal. In the
North, those that have to do with reason, action, and concrete reality
are accented; in the South, those that concern sensibility, feeling,
and form. Since these elements are complementary, the ideal would
be for both cultures to perfect themselves through each emulating
what the other has of positive worth. This would be the balance, the
synthesis to which the cultural frontier invites us.

Imbalance and Tension

Nowadays it would be very risky to affirm that this interpenetration is taking place. Instead one would have to speak of a penetration
in favor of the North American middle culture and particularly of the
values that are peculiar to it. This is due, of course, to the greater

"clout" that these values are given by the general technical efficiency of that great country aided by its advertising and its economic
and political power.

It is happening not only in America. The European countries al-
lied with the United States on the present world frontier comment
sometimes with irritation, other times with irony, on the penetration
of the Yankee way of life—what they call there the "cocacolization"
of Europe. Obviously, such a skin-deep penetration is not in itself
serious, especially for nations with an already mature culture. The
danger for the rest of us is that this influence—limited, I repeat, to
the peculiar values and not the universal ones—may be the breach
through which the innermost character and personality of our peoples comes to be affected.

In our America, the contagion of these excesses of the United
States is relatively recent. During the past century, when the great
Sarmiento came even to the point of advocating our imitating the
United States rather than Spain, his recommendation did not receive
any significant attention in our zones of middle culture. At the end of
the century, the situation began reversing itself. While the Yankee
influences grew among our bourgeoisie, the intellectual minorities
took up positions in defense of the national calling; that is to say,
they watched over the collective destiny belonging to Latin America.
This is the deep purpose not only of the deliberately ideological and
polemical positions, those of Martí, González Prada, and Rodó, as
well as of the more harsh and elemental anti-Americanism, the attitude of Vargas Vila, Ugarte, and Blanco Fombona, but also of the
more direct intellectual and aesthetic attitudes, those of modernism
in general. Corresponding to the same spirit is the movement that
Pedro Henríquez Ureña characterized as the search for our expressive mode: the more or less indigenous "nativism," or Afro-creolism,
of our islands. This search is also revealed in the "westernizing" arguments of an Alfonso Reyes, and even in the conversion—or, if you
will, the reversion—of José Vasconcelos, whose revolutionary radi-
calism and contemplation of "the cosmic race" finally gave way to a
conservative mystique with strong hispanicizing emphases. In every
case it was a matter of the sensitive and watchful intellectual minority coming out in defense of the special vocation of our peoples—
sometimes not without some injustice toward the Yankee.

Thus we have set forth the basic problem that deepens and in-
tensifies on the cultural frontier. On the one hand, the middle culture
of Latin America, although still greatly inhibited by its "primary
loyalties," nevertheless tends to become perverted, incorporating
Northern culture indiscriminately, admitting its particularities more

than its universal values. On the other hand, our most representative minorities, zealous for their own image, tend to reject the North outright, feeding on their own substance, which they season at most with European universal essences. Thus there is an imbalance toward the external and a tension in the internal: a conflict between interest in the foreign and in the provincial. Are we obliged to accept a situation that poses such a dilemma? This is the question that I would like to be able to answer in the next and final lecture.

V

The Contemporary

Situation

on the Frontier

In the duality of American cultures, the frontier occupies an extreme position, which is at the same time one of risk and of privilege. On the one hand, the respective repertories of ideas, cutoms, and life patterns confront one another on it. The predominance of the North, and the fact that its values enjoy the greater currency of which I spoke earlier, make that zone of contact an unbalanced frontier, both in the cultural order and in the political and economic orders as well. The weaker region is instinctively on the defensive, and its resistance is constantly threatened. In addition to the external pressure, its own inanities and its tendencies to accommodation and limitation conspire against it. These do not always arise from the mass of the people. Besides, among the ordinary people there tends to operate a kind of inertia of customs that preserves what Ortega calls "primary loyalties."

On the other hand, the classes with "interests" and with a fair amount of education are the ones that through snobbishness or by deliberation most easily fall into the imitation of the manners and customs of the alien power. For their part, the cultural elite with the best education or with the greatest sensitivity vacillate between the primary loyalties and the utilitarian pressure that bids them serve the most immediate and concrete interests. Generally, it is a struggle between sentiment and reason, between tradition and innovation. When the border is that of a well-integrated national territory, the latter provides sufficient powers of resistance. When this is not the case, the frontier finds itself in a "limit situation"—if I may be allowed to borrow the concept from a certain existentialist philosophy —and oscillates between the inanities of certain people and the

74

anxieties of others who feel called upon to safeguard the common destiny.

But I said that this frontier situation is also one of privilege. It is so in the sense that, precisely because it is presented with this challenge, it has the opportunity to take advantage of it as an element of stimulation. Thus, too, frontiers resolve dilemma-producing tensions through a high historical sense, equally distant from crude antagonism and submissive collaborationism, that is, through a sense neither provincial nor narrowly nationalistic, but human and universal.

I have already established, in considering the dimensions of culture, that they may apply to internal social segments within a single nation or to a homogeneous constellation of nations. Thus, in Latin America today there are residual areas of primitive indigenous cultures and of imported ones of African origin, as marginal or subordinate as you please, but not for all that less particularized in their attitudes, beliefs, and customs. On a higher level there is a vast area of middle culture directly derived from the Spanish, though embellished by racial intermixture and by the American physical environment. Finally, as the high flowering of the dominant part, there are our minorities, in whose select culture loyalty to the American is modified by the most diverse hemispheric and "western" influences with a universal accent. Looked at carefully, the culture of Latin America is not yet a homogeneous unity. It is in process of amalgamation.

This is taking place much less in the United States. There the middle culture—with English roots, but greatly nourished by other migratory European ingredients—embraces the entire nation. In the North, the primitive elements never had the will to culture and do not count. For its part, the intellectual minority, though of great value, weighs less than that of Latin America in the formation of the national culture. In short, the culture of the United States is of the middle class, very integrated and standardized.

Thus, when we speak of the cultural frontier between the two Americas, the question cannot be over-simplified. To what contacts and to what oppositions are we referring? With what part or parts of Latin American culture does that of the United States establish a relation of tangency? Furthermore, what reality, after all, does this cultural frontier have, if by it is understood not a mere separation, but a confluence and coexistence?

This last question is one that above all we must clear up at once. Let us not forget that the frontier is made of the two contiguous zones that it separates. Concretely, the zone on the side of the North is quite ambiguous in the continental section. That is, in the southern part of the United States, the border is saturated with traditions and demographic elements of Indian and Mexican origin. In some places the zone still remains that disturbed fringe to which we referred earlier--a zone of adventure, contraband, and freedom from other inhibitions. Perhaps it would be giving it too much honor to call this a *cultural* frontier. With respect to the maritime wing, the reality is scarcely less equivocal and unstable. In large measure what comes to our shores from the United States is a swarm of tourists, business agents, and transient impresarios, and the elements of our population that come into contact with that oscillating tide tend also to be the least typical of us. In Cuba, it is notorious to what point the North American colony, generally people of moderate cultural level, lives—or, we will rather say *lived*—as if encysted, on the margin of the Cuban essence. I believe this happens much less in Puerto Rico, but I suspect not enough less so that one could speak of the frontier as a contact between the respectively most characteristic elements of both cultural regions.

One would have to ask himself if, strictly speaking, this cultural frontier is not still just the physical junction for an active confluence of cultures rather than a profound reality. Would these then be the middle cultures of North and Latin America, or only those of the most select minorities that are elevated over them? Finally, we Puerto Ricans and Cubans would have to ask ourselves resolutely if we really can consider ourselves, in our middle culture, as genuine representatives of all Hispanic America. Is what we call our cultural frontier ours only or that of all our republics?

Within this complex of questions—which we would not now be able by any means to unravel completely—we could nevertheless not advance one step without venturing the core of a hypothesis, even though it is not possible at this time to substantiate it fully, because instead of a lecture, that would require a book. My working thesis would be that the mission of a frontier is two-fold. On the one hand, it serves as a "confine," containing within the area it outlines the peculiar essences that constitute what is different in its personality, the legitimate objects of its self-regard. It is its service on behalf of dignity, in defense of which every risk must be faced, without on that account requiring the assumption of offensively arrogant attitudes. On the other hand, it is the task of the frontier to afford to the people or peoples behind it the opportunity to contemplate, not in the abstract but by means of an experience of interpenetration, the relative worth of two distinct repertories of values. This advantage follows from one people's adopting from their neighbors the universal values perhaps missing from their own culture. This is its function of communication. Thus, the frontier fails equally when it is shut with dogmatic and provincial hostility and when, due to the opposite excess, it is abandoned to that sort of systematic alienation that we call a sellout.

It must rather serve as a sifter or balance for values. It has customs offices and customs duties to regulate the import of merchandise. It also needs sensitive cultural mechanisms designed to discriminate between the intangibles that deserve to be welcomed and those that do not. This cannot be left to the mercy of the imitative tendencies that originate in simple admiration, snobbism, or crude interest. Such spontaneous movements, more frequent in the favored classes than among the common people, tend to welcome from the alien culture not the universal, but the peculiar and distinctive; not the perennial, but the current. This is why active guidance—discreet but continuous—is so necessary, using all of the agencies capable of influencing what the people receive, such as institutions of instruction, the press, cultural associations, and in general, all of the channels through which intelligence operates. The method of such action is the dialogue.

Long ago I read a little French novel that I remember vividly. It was from the pen of the great Catholic humanist Pierre Lasserre and it was entitled *La Promenade Insolite*, "The Unusual Stroll." It was the story of how a small town in France was always in a state of tension because of the rivalry between its two most representative citizens, the priest and the local freethinker. The rancor between them was as deep as it was circumspect. But one winter afternoon without noticing one another, each independently sat down on a bench in the town square to enjoy the sun. They remained there for some time without speaking or even looking at each other. Finally, some minor incident that I do not recall—perhaps both were distributing crumbs to the birds—obliged them to enter into small talk. When the birds left, they continued talking. The sun went down and they set out walking together in animated conversation. They went on strolling and chatting for a long time. As the shadows of night fell, the astonished neighbors saw them return from the outskirts of the town walking arm in arm. Neither had convinced the other. But in some way, as a result of that conversation, of that unusual stroll, there was no longer so much rancor between the supporters of the freethinker and those of the priest. The dialogue had wrought the miracle.

America and Puerto Rico

I am not going to dwell on the obvious lesson. I only want to apply it to our America without giving it overdue weight or emphasis.

Our hemisphere is divided between the freethinker and the priest, that is to say, between Anglo-Saxon rationality and Latin sensibility, between the realm of sobriety, where it is enough that friends shake hands, and that of demonstrativeness, where the embrace is the law of friendship. It is of great importance for America and for the whole world—above all for the world of Western values—that these two great areas of culture not only comprehend each other but that they establish real mutuality. It is important that each of them preserve its particular values and emulate the universal values of the other.

The frontier is a field of experimentation for such understanding. Through its example it will exert an influence over the rest of America. I mean that the rest of our nations will give an account of inter-American relations according to how these relations have fared on the frontier. Thus it bears a great responsibility. If it is demonstrated that in this zone of greatest contact the North American influence wreaks havoc, destroying the finest values of our race, the division between the Americas will become deeper and irredeemable. If, on the other hand, it becomes evident that the closest association with the world of the North not only has left these values unharmed but has enriched our civilization with meanings that are both technical and human, this experience of ours will serve to stimulate firmer relations between the two Americas.

It has been said that Puerto Rico is the bridge between these two cultures. I know the word does not please you. A bridge is something over which people walk, and you rightly would not want to bear the impress of wayfarers' feet. I propose rather to say to you that this whole area we somewhat vaguely call the Caribbean is like the town square of the hemisphere, and that, if the Mexican frontier is a sort of trench, across which nevertheless fears and suspicions are increasingly being dissipated, the Antilles are benches that invite relaxation and dialogue.

It has been Puerto Rico's lot to be the most accessible in this meeting of cultures, not because of geography but by accident of history.

Love of Self, Imitation, Emulation

In what we might call the experience of frontiers in general, certain attitudes corresponding to basic psychological capacities are usually operative, either conjointly or separately.

One of them is love of self. Like all living beings, humans tend to preserve and reproduce themselves; they differ from the rest in that they are aware of this necessity and satisfy it deliberately. They know what is proper to them and they defend it. The Stoics saw the

root of the feeling of human dignity in the consciousness of rationality. But this concern for what is one's own extends to the entire
domain of human strivings. Man loves everything that is his own,
and he does not stop—at least without compulsion—to consider if
what is peculiarly his is also meritorious. Apart from individuals who
have fallen into total decadence, every human being defends his own
personality.

Well then, this psychic state also extends itself in more diffuse
form to collective individuals, to peoples and races or constellations
of related peoples. Even the most primitive people fight not only for
their property but to preserve their ways and customs. To the degree
that a nation or a race in the course of history enriches its consciousness and its spiritual patrimony, this feeling grows. Love of self
changes into pride. From this springs, in the last analysis, the affirmation of collective personality that we call patriotism. The importance of this love of self is therefore enormous, for good and for ill.
Certain utopians may dream of a world in which only superior beings
and peoples are found; but what the scrutiny of history shows us is
that no people resigns itself even to the thought of being absorbed by
another, regardless of how much superiority it might recognize in the
other. Even when political formulas designed to incorporate one nation into another are advocated, care is always taken to allege,
though with doubtful validity, that this would not mean the loss of
the thus absorbed nation's own personality.

As a source of the national spirit, the collective love of self tends
to be the most profound reason why nations at times find it so difficult to comprehend and cooperate with one another, and why in international politics the most reasonable and universally relevant en-
deavors run aground or are frustrated. Like all love, including that of
country, it may at times be blind.

Another of the elemental psychic states to which I referred before operates to a certain extent in the opposite direction. I refer to
the instinct of adaptation, which often stimulates the imitation of
others. If love of self is conservative and tends to preserve one's own
integrity, this other movement of the individual or collective spirit is
outwardly and receptively oriented, as if seeking substances with
which to fill an interior emptiness. In the individual order, we observe it particularly in children. In the collective, it is characteristic
of young nations. It appears, in effect, that this porosity may be necessary for development itself.

I do not believe that what is called the decline of the West is yet
a reality, but if such a thing some day comes to pass, surely one of its
causes could be a certain excess of accumulated arrogance, a certain

shutting of Europe into the castle of its own riches. Probably not at all unrelated to this is the well-known and almost systematic displeasure with which Europe is wont to contemplate its offspring across the Atlantic, particularly the United States. Youthfulness, which for everyone is "the heavenly treasure," is envied just as much as is power. Nevertheless, I repeat that one of the marks of this youthfulness, at least in its early stages, is usually the tendency to imitate more mature peoples.

These two tendencies of which I am speaking generally become most marked in regions adjacent to an unbalanced frontier, creating in them a tension similar to that of islands, of which we spoke earlier. Note how it is impossible to overemphasize the importance of psychology in international relations, particularly across unbalanced frontiers. For the same reason, the problem of good relations—which always arises in times of crisis or changes in government—has as a basic datum the knowledge of the character and the values of the nations that the frontier separates. Needless to say, all the efforts to resolve such a problem with economic formulas, or with mere agreements between governments without reference to the feelings of the people, are generally condemned to pathetic failure.

The collective love of self is found with particular sensitivity on the frontier, but yet—I hope this does not seem contradictory or ambivalent—these frontier regions, when they are located next to a powerful nation, are also the most exposed to the inconstancies of imitation that I mentioned earlier. Naturally they feel more directly the impact of the influences proceeding from the neighbor; but in addition, the resistance to economic and cultural, and even at times political, influences tends to be weaker, and the very confluence of heterogeneous elements helps to relax this resistance.

Today I should like to make the case for the desideratum that seems to me to follow from these considerations about the sensitivity of the frontier. The two psychic movements that I have been referring to—love of self and imitation—lead respectively to equally undesirable extreme patterns. Love of self tends to be inert and purely defensive. We all know that one makes no real progress without recognizing superior worth wherever it may be found, and for that reason Goethe says in his *Wilhelm Meister* that the essence of education is the cult and cultivation of respect. The consciousness of our own worth, which is self-respect, must be united with esteem for the worth of others and with the will to emulate their genuine merit to enrich our own. On the other hand, too easy a deference toward the other power weakens our own personality. If excess love of self is conducive to a crude provincialism that retards our development, imitation leads us to that form of self-annihilation that we call a sellout.

Luckily these two psychic movements can mutually interact and limit one another, as in a dialectical synthesis, giving way to a productive attitude: emulation. To emulate is to imitate the other with the purpose of surpassing him or at least of equalling him. Thus, it presupposes esteem, neither immoderate nor blind, for one's own abilities. In the presence of the situation of inferiority that an unbalanced frontier proclaims and emphasizes, there is only one worthy solution: The weaker human area must realize its maximum effort to remove the disparity.

The Special Case of Puerto Rico

And now I should like your special permission to discuss, with all possible delicacy, because it concerns matters that touch you to the quick, the case of Puerto Rico. This is the very model of the frontier theme, and not to approach it specifically, having already talked about it so much in general terms, would not only be an unpardonable omission but an offensive evasion. Beyond this, I should like to make it very clear from the start—and I will say why in a moment— that I am not going to allow myself any intrusion of a definitive nature in what this question involves in the purely political order, that is, in what concerns the constitutional status that Puerto Rico should have. This is a matter that is entirely up to you Puerto Ricans to decide—although naturally the rest of us, deep inside, may have particular preferences. What really is indispensable is that when we consider the problem as such we look at it without reservations and with all the facts.

The question presents two aspects that it is first well to consider separately, with the intention of later trying to integrate them. One of them is that of the exact relation Puerto Rico has with the rest of America, and this implies determining if it really is a frontier and in what sense. The other aspect is internal to Puerto Rico itself. What problems and what prospects does the peculiarity of this situation create for the island? Both aspects stem from a single central fact that in turn is characterized by a certain duality.

As we said earlier, all islands situated close to an intense focus of political and economic power with which they cannot compete generally find themselves subject to a special tension. Once they are of appreciable size, the very condition of insularity infuses in them a certain detachment and a kind of vocation to independence. But on the other hand, the power vortex exerts an absorbing attraction on them. Being situated advantageously for commerce, they find themselves dangerously exposed politically. And this is so not only because of the external forces exerted on them, but also because of the special domestic interests that always tend to associate themselves with those forces. Only a very effective effort by those with the most alert consciences can prevent the existence of a great deal of wrong in the conduct of these insular societies and can save their destiny— we shall presently see what I mean by this word—from being compromised. Needless to say, this is the case with my own country. Certain transformations in its history—including the present one, which could not be more painful—are explainable in large part as sporadic efforts, not always prudent in their procedures, to affirm in such circumstances an absolute nationalism that is always susceptible to being converted into a nationalist absolutism.

Although free from such risks at the present time, the case of Puerto Rico does not cease to be fundamentally more difficult, due to a greater ambiguity. Here is a relatively small island compared to the other larger ones of the Antilles, and for this reason less favored than they with natural resources, but much denser in population. The people of this island are of ethnic composition similar to that of Cuba and the Dominican Republic. Its tradition, its customs, and its culture have deep Spanish roots. For all spiritual purposes, Puerto Rico is a piece of Hispanic America.

Very well, onto this people was imposed a political link as the result of, as we all know, an historical event that was, in reality, more an abrupt and sudden occurrence than a natural process. This link, which Puerto Ricans could not have anticipated and about which they were not consulted nor their consent received, was from the beginning invested with no juridical formality but was constituted as a bare fact of military and governmental occupation. From such obvious antecedents stems the duality—more than that, the radical contradiction—that lies at the base of the Puerto Rican problem. The modifications that have been made subsequently in this situation, particularly those that relate to the juridico-political character of the link, are important, as we shall now see, but not enough to alter the linkage itself in its essence.

We could say, then, that both Puerto Rico's soul and body are outside the borders of the United States; but at the same time she finds herself in an historical situation that tends to sever these two parts of her being—to unite her in spirit with the nation to the north, while her body remains among us as a mere geographical testimony to her Hispanic-American past.

Under these circumstances, it is in order to ask ourselves, provisionally, up to what point Puerto Rico really is a frontier and in what sense. For we have already seen that the condition for such is not only contiguity but also *opposition,* or confronting of interests. And assuming she were in reality a frontier, one would have to ask of what type it is. Is it one of Latin America with the United States or of the United States with Latin America?

These questions are far from idle. It is no secret that the doubts implicit in them determine not a few attitudes in our America—generally the most superficial ones. Some suppose that Puerto Rico has voluntarily "sold out" to the United States with a sort of lackey obsequiousness; others regard it with pity, as a land subjugated by "Yankee imperialism." For the former, it is now merely the frontier land of the North's perimeter; for the latter, it is our unredeemed zone, Little Red Riding Hood who has strayed into the terrain of the wolf and who must now be saved from the consequences of her own innocence. These refer to what is outside or comes from the outside. And on the inside, how can we deny that the conflict between the Hispanic tradition and the political link generates, among yourselves, a whole group of tensions and equivocations, or hesitations with respect to the present and the future, that disturb the Puerto Rican soul with concern about its proper destiny?

It would be very foolish to dismiss such serious questions lightly, but in some manner it is necessary to clear them up at the outset in order not to get lost in their very complexity. I would say, on the basis of general considerations already set forth, and allowing for later qualifications, that Puerto Rico is really a frontier, not for the simple reason of the geographical location she shares with the other islands of the Greater Antilles, but on account of something more essential: the forces of opposition and resistance that are *still* rooted in her history and culture. I would add that this persistent reality makes her *yet* a frontier of Latin America looking to the north, and not the inverse; that she is not *now* a political frontier, since she does not have a sovereignty separate from the United States; nor *yet* an economic frontier, since she does not represent a constellation of interests distinct from those of the North, or even indifferent to the latter; but she is indeed a cultural frontier *sui generis.* In her the ways of life and thought of the United States communicate closely and enter into quite intimate confluence with those of Hispanic-American culture.

Finally, if I had to anticipate what is the great general problem of Puerto Rico, I would venture to say that it revolves around the way in which the adverbs of time that I have just used deliberately to suggest a certain transitoriness are to be resolved. If, far from being provisional or merely passing, the situations to which they point become definitively consolidated, the problem is reduced to asking to what point the cultural frontier will be able to stand up against the non-existence of a political frontier or an economic frontier. I hope some light may be thrown on all of this by the considerations to which the other aspect of the case of Puerto Rico lends itself: the internal one.

The colonial history of Puerto Rico was characterized by an almost unswerving loyalty to the mother country. I have heard not a few Puerto Ricans comment on this with a certain contrition, as if to suggest that this people lacked the courage of rebellion. Without any great authority to dissent, since I am far from being well informed about your history, I venture my impression that this suggestion is too harsh. If it were in order to apply to a people classificatory concepts proper to individual psychology, we could say that Puerto Rico is much more introverted—yes, just that—than, for example, any of the other Antilles that became republics, and it is now known that the energies of this type of character are not easily articulated with those of others. They are not generally exuberant or explosive, but are concentrated in order to be distributed later in a flowing and continuous manner.

On the other hand, although the colony of Puerto Rico suffered its share of abuses and cruelties at the hands of Spain, I also have the impression that because of the greater gentleness of the Puerto Rican the mother country did not carry its harshness here as far as it did in Cuba, for example. Nor was Puerto Rico as exposed to subversive incitations coming from outside. Your separatist leaders seem to have conceived that ideal as a viable one only as a function of the independence of Cuba, and this not because of any second-string spirit—one must not forget that the shout of Lares preceded that of Baire*—but because of the clear realization of how difficult it would be for Puerto Rico, given her geographical smallness and her unusual isolation, to make a liberating effort effective completely on her own. Cuba itself took almost a century longer than the continental colonies to free herself. It is for this reason that the joint independence of Cuba and Puerto Rico was insisted on so strongly by Martí, and perhaps this thinking also dominated Hostos's dream for an Antilles confederation.

If, in spite of men like Hostos, Betances, Baldorioty de Castro, and Ruiz Belvis, your history manifests a persistent fidelity to Spain, this only proves how much affection you have for the values of that land and what a tremendous shock it must have represented for your collective consciousness to see yourselves suddenly transferred, without your choosing it and as a consequence of a war in which you

---

*Baire in Cuba and Lares in Puerto Rico are the towns from which their country's cry for independence from Spain is considered to have first been sounded.—Tr.

had not taken part, to another sovereignty and to a cultural sphere ruled by very different values.

Your very loyalty to the mother country perhaps contributed to the fact that this link did not carry with it any differential treatment or concessions for Puerto Rico. The Philippines received promises even before Aguinaldo exacted them. For Cuba, the Platt Amendment was at least imposed as an appendix to a constitution the Cuban people themselves created. Puerto Rico, where for good or for ill the autonomy granted by Spain was then in force, was not recognized by the Treaty of Paris as an entity in its own right, but as an object of the right of the stronger, the right of dominion.

From this zero point in esteem by the other, or more precisely from the initial point of clash between the dignity that you felt as an Hispanic people and that which was denied you by the expeditious political mechanics with which it is customary to wind up wars, Puerto Rico had to face up to the future. At one and the same time she had to renew her history and to reform it: to remain faithful to herself, and at the same time in some fashion to assimilate the new circumstances. Whoever does not take account of this problem will not be able to appreciate the difficulties it involved and what Puerto Rico has done to solve it.

Everything then led to the fear that the historical forces bearing down on the island would soon reveal to the Hispanic world that Puerto Rico was to be excluded forever from its spiritual domain. To be sure, there were the accumulation of primary loyalties that are generally embodied in popular customs, and the steadfast and uncompromising leadership of some eminent personalities; there was a resistance movement, as we say now. But the factors of pressure and compulsion seemed pervasive, and all worked in the direction of increasingly "Americanizing" this great rock that stood guard over the entrance to the American Mediterranean. Some of these factors were spiritual in nature: The official orientation of public instruction called for compulsory teaching of English as the principal language in the schools. Others were of a material nature: The conversion of the traditional economy of Puerto Rico, which was no doubt weak and sluggish but not without a certain exuberance of Acadian charms, into a crass extractive economy based on large domestic and foreign capital investments, on the concentration of agrarian property, and on the large scale semi-industrialization of sugar, linked to the market of the United States.

These forces, I repeat, seemed enslaving and irresistible. For nearly a half century after the North American occupation, the tone of Puerto Rican life according to your own witnesses was one of deep discouragement. You felt as though you had no pulse, that you were caught in an inexorable destiny.

With memories of his revolutionary activity in Mexico still fresh and at the full height of his influence as an educator of America, José Vasconcelos visited this island, and all of us admired the firmness with which he exhorted the youth of Puerto Rico to open the way for her independence at whatever cost. Today one wonders if, along with the courage, there may not also have been a bit of unconscious cruelty in that exhortation—if it was not like mentioning the rope in the home of one who was hanged, or more exactly, like treating as feasible, though with heroism, something that at the time there were reasons to consider impossible. To me personally, it is evident that this urging, coupled with the example of Ireland, had much to do with the budding of certain plans for resolving the problem of Puerto Rico through naked violence.

The very disparity between the recommended cure and the experienced reality helped to accentuate the feeling of frustration that it aimed to remove. Implicitly or explicitly, your literature and other arts reflected this feeling. All of the poetry of José de Diego breathed a sort of sweet nostalgia for unrealized ideals. In the poetry of Lloréns Torres about the land and its customs, there was a kind of wounded love, a devitalized idealization. Destined at the height of his young manhood to a tragic, untimely end, Antonio Pedreira made an inventory of collective failures, though not without ending up with a passionate hope. A little later one heard the ironic epithet of Palés Matos: "Puerto Rico, good-for-nothing."

The popular music also expressed this profound disquietude, barely disguised in the exquisite *danzas* of Morel Campos, which seemed to exude a sort of dispirited lassitude. Still during the 1930s, finding myself in an informal meeting of Latins in the United States, a few melancholy Puerto Ricans in attendance were urged to sing something typical of their island. They sang a sort of hillbilly number the theme of which was the Guanica sugar refinery. I shall never be able to forget the deep affliction of that melody, intermixed with obvious civic resentments. And it is a fact that when a feeling of frustration dominates the life of a people, it begins by clipping the wings of politics itself, transforming it into political maneuvering, into the vociferous clash of partisan factions, above whose pettiness a few exemplary figures are barely able to elevate themselves. I repeat: In that moment, Puerto Rico appeared to have lost all hope for her own destiny.

Destiny! Here is a concept so worked over that it behooves us to refurbish it so that it will not overly burden us as individuals and nations. Generally destiny is spoken of in a mystical sense, if you will permit the word, in a sense reminiscent of that concept of fate or of inevitable doom that the Greeks revealed in their tragedies. As a matter reserved for the will of the gods, destiny thus turned out to be ineluctible and inescapable for human beings. Only the humanism of Greece won the freedom to see destiny as pure contingency, pure "luck," the good or evil meaning of which lay hidden in the bosom of the future.

But if destiny means that, it is not worth discussing: Wait for it, that is all. Fortunately, a more reasonable conception is possible, and this is the one that simply understands it as a cross or adjustment between what a person desires and what is possible, or if one prefers to express it in Ortega's terminology, between man and his circumstances. As to inevitability, it is surely enough that we cannot always choose our circumstances. But what we can always choose is our action in the face of them. The history of a nation is made up not only of the things that it does, but also of the things that it suffers because it has not been able to avoid them. Thus, it is not completely responsible for its history. One can only ask it to account for what it does with the part over which it can exercise its will, and to the extent that it knows how to do so profitably one can say that it carves out its own destiny.

The Overcoming

What mysterious forces—mysterious sometimes because of their unexpected existence, at other times because of the imponderable and unforeseeable character of their operation—are the ones then that come to the rescue of the destiny of nations? Is it the invisible accumulation of that "intra-historical" consciousness of which Unamuno spoke? Is it the simple renewal of the generations, each of which inaugurates its distinctive powers and hopes? Or is it simply, in the case of a youthful people, the marvel of its own vitality?

What is certain is that the spiritual reserves of Puerto Rico overcame the feeling of frustration of which I was speaking. I visited the island for the first time in 1941, in connection with a writers' congress held under the auspices of this university, and I then felt some innovative gusts in the air. The young people whom Pedreira had exhorted to such ardent hopes in his book *Insularity* had not forgotten the noble lesson that had risen from his analysis of the wrongs done to their island. A spirit of impatience, clearly moved by the ideal of independence, was already virtually at battle pitch, and the colonial governing power seemed to me already on the defensive.

A few years later, invited to the installation ceremony for the first governor of Puerto Rico, I returned to visit San Juan. That spirit had intensified. During those very days a strenuous campaign for seats in the legislature was in progress. I attended a meeting in which for the first time I heard Luis Muñoz Marín speak. With simple but extremely effective eloquence he depicted the misery of an island that was overpopulated and lacking in resources; he denounced the complicity of foreign interests with certain domestic interests; he made it clear to his listeners that the remedy for these evils lay in the hands of the people, simply by faithfully exercising their right to vote; finally, he exhorted them to remount the slope down which they had been sliding. And by the light of stars and candlesticks, I could see in the faces of those who were listening a glow of determination and faith.

The one thing I did not come to this platform to do was to deliver political panegyrics. But, as my noble fellow countryman whom I have quoted so much, wrote: "He who honors is honored." I would feel ashamed if out of excessive discretion in the face of inevitable party divisions I were to silence my tribute to one of the Latin Americans in whom the most perceptive observers of our nations have recognized the stature of a statesman. Nobility, so untypical of politicians, has distinguished the work of your Muñoz Marín. This man, who began in the literary field by writing poetry, later continued his creative effort in history and produced a two-fold work. Internally, he made possible an enormous task of economic reconstruction, in which the island has seen itself raised out of its own weakness by its "bootstraps" so as to achieve an astonishing level of prosperity within a few years. Externally, he lifted Puerto Rico from its indefinite status as a mere territory, to give it a higher level of dignity in respect to its relations with the United States. Without foolishly defiant attitudes, with only the weapons of imagination, intelligence, diplomatic tact, and persuasive patience, Muñoz Marín has brought about a veritable revolution in Puerto Rico, in the most positive and substantial sense of that well-worn word.

He has not been alone, of course. In this enterprise of increasingly widening Puerto Rico's horizons, he was accompanied from the beginning by men of distinction. Of these, now that I am afforded this opportunity for public homage, I will only mention one who seems to me eminently representative: none other than the rector of this university. It is my duty to recall what you know better than I: that Muñoz Marín in this period of Puerto Rican history has embodied the affirmation of the political consciousness and the social and material prosperity of his nation, and that Jaime Benítez is one of the most responsible representatives of the development of its cultural consciousness. Under his inspiration and that of others before and after him, Puerto Rico recovered the right to give preferential status to her language, that noble coin that each race mints for its spiritual commerce and for the determination and exchange of its values. The school system was fruitfully broadened, and like a modest river that finally empties into a deep estuary of wide dimensions, it has produced this university, which today is the pride of America.

Your entire culture has been undergoing purification through such influences. In your everyday customs you have been able to resist the surge of "little Yankeeism" that a few years ago it seemed was going to drown you. There is still widespread imitation of the foreigner on the superficial levels of the snob culture, which everywhere welcomes him; but your deep levels of feeling and thought remain intact and even accentuate the traditional. For example, we were agreeably surprised last Christmas to see how much the famous tradition of Christmas carols and holiday gifts still survives, held with deep affection by your people as part of the pattern of life in many homes.

It is true that the common speech suffers at every turn from the inevitable spatterings of bilingualism, and I believe that this is going to require a whole campaign of purification. But in the realm of the most thoughtful culture there is a great increase in what is essentially the element of devotion—devotion to the noblest in taste and expression. Your literature is rising above provincial delight in the mere peculiarities of stylization to the eager contemplation of universal values. When it seemed that your people were already in danger of seduction by alien styles of life, your poets and prose writers came forth saying, in energetic prose or in ironic verse, that doing and having are enterprises in which men can imitate one another with impunity, but that one cannot renounce what is his own without being a counterfeiter. One of these prose writers, Pedreira, whom I shall never tire of recalling and always with melancholy devotion, cited in *Insularity* the solemn sentence that Rosendo Matienzo Cintrón had written in 1903: "Today Puerto Rico is only a crowd. But when the crowd has a soul, then Puerto Rico will be a country." Well then, I believe that today it can be said, not that Puerto Rico has her soul, but that she has recovered it.

But then I will be asked: "Is all now well here? Is there no Puerto Rican problem?" Yes, there surely is, and it can even be said that this problem is possibly more acute than ever. More acute because it is more subtle, because it is more complex.

Before suggesting why, I should like to rescue from an apparent ambiguity not only what I am going to add now, but many other earlier judgments made in the lectures I am now concluding. Reality, like landscapes, does not usually present a simple color, but blends of colors. In the human domain above all it abounds in contrasts, in changeable tints, and even in incongruities, and for this reason paradox is so often the most adequate literary device for coping with it. Goethe was fond of saying that genuine reflection begins when we say: "Yes, but . . ." This is particularly the case when one is dealing with ambiguous realities, with indecisive or conflictive situations, like that of Puerto Rico. I was saying that here there is a more acute problem than ever before. Paradoxically it derives from your very prosperity, from your very progress in all spheres, including the political sphere.

I have just paid tribute to the vigor with which Puerto Rico overcame the crisis of colonial domination. In all fairness I feel obliged to recognize the cooperation of another factor working in the same direction: the substantial change in the policy of the United States toward Latin America and toward Puerto Rico in particular. For whatever reasons, and I believe it is principally because of that flowering of the ethical consciousness of the United States to which I referred in previous lectures, from the second Roosevelt until now, North American policy toward our America has become more and more considerate and sympathetic. The very conception of the "good neighbor" gave a new meaning to the frontier. It is no accident that during more or less the same years the Dominican Republic ceased being a field for dragooning by the Marines—although unfortunately the ill-fated republic became a fief of domestic despotism—the Platt Amendment was abolished in Cuba, and not much later Puerto Rico gained the position of dignity that she now has in her relations with the United States.

Is the rest of our America well aware of what this changed relationship means? This change, due to Puerto Rico's efforts as well as to the good will of the North, has had the effect of completely undermining the statement that this is one of the "irredentist" lands, like Ireland or the former Alsace and Lorraine and like others of today that we all know—poor lands with subjugated will, with unheeded cry, without any alternatives save abject submission or desperate violence. In internal affairs, Puerto Rico today enjoys civil and democratic liberties like few republics of our America. In external affairs, she can be independent when she wishes to be, when it is to her advantage to be. Thus, hers is not one more case of the classical imperial-colonial relation. Strictly speaking, neither is hers fundamentally a political problem. If the Puerto Ricans can resolve it, as I understand they can, simply with a plebiscite that declares their will one way or the other, the problem is simply one of ranking their own desires, of determining what type of interests are the most important and which are the least. In short, it is a problem of value judgments.

It is precisely this that makes the problem most difficult. For it is a question of incommensurable value judgments, in the sense that they cannot be subject to a single criterion, since some are of a spiritual and cultural order, that is, of the order of sensibility, and others are of a material order. Even though these material values are the preferred objects of attention by the prudential and rational faculties, they do not on that account have any less effect on spiritual necessities and expedients, since we all know that even elevated interests and values of this type grow or decline depending on whether or not they can count on a solid economic base to support them. In sum, the complexion of the Puerto Rican problem has changed. Put a bit harshly, it consists of seeing herself obliged to decide if she is to choose her political and economic orientation by reference to her culture, or if, on the contrary, she is to accept the culture that political and economic expedients impose on her.

In the face of such a problem of insightful value appraisal, in which what is at stake is nothing less than the future of your society, it would be unpardonable meddling for any foreigner, no matter how great might be the love he professes for this land, to assume an advisory stance or even to offer casual impressions. And I want to repeat how lamentable it is that many of our Latin American fellows, in referring to the case of Puerto Rico, choose an attitude of commiseration, if not one of irony, instead of weighing the seriousness of the problem and all that Puerto Rico has done and continues to do to solve it with a maximum both of dignity and of advantage.

Having said this, no one can help observing, on the other side, the series of tensions that the problem poses for Puerto Ricans themselves. We will begin with the *historical* tension. History is not only that which one has lived through, but also that which, on the basis of this experience, one should be able to live through in the future. This type of continuity is compromised here, or at least is in serious danger. As a nation with an Hispanic constitution and tradition, Puerto Rico sees herself driven by circumstances, including her very economic development, toward detaching herself more and more from her own antecedents, to the point of running the risk of one day finding her soul in the "spiritual abode" of our race and her body "on the side of the infidels." Such a mistake engenders a *psychological* tension between primary and profound loyalties and adventitious demands, which tend to undermine these loyalties because of the tremendous force that the immediate always has in comparison with the merely traditional. Accordingly there is also manifest a *cultural* tension, between the preservation of the people's own personality and the prospect of a growing loss of character; between the resistance that love of self and honor stimulate and the imitative temptation that contact with a more "current" and efficient culture arouses even in the best informed or most favored social classes.

These tensions are in reality those that underlie Puerto Rico's political problem: the polemic between statehood, protected autonomy, or absolute independence. And since every tension between human motivations contains a dramatic element, it is no great exaggeration to speak of the drama of Puerto Rico—a drama that does not cease being so, but rather becomes accentuated, by the many who do not perceive it or adopt toward it a resigned or careless attitude. Fortunately, this is no longer the attitude most representative of the contemporary Puerto Rican consciousness. Puerto Rico has found her soul. It is still a soul unsure of its destiny, but it is a soul concerned about it.

Adventure in Prophecy

Well now, do these tensions of which I have just spoken represent true dilemmas, or on the contrary, are they generated between goals that are capable of reconciliation? This definitely seems to me to be the great question that hovers over Puerto Rico. If I were at liberty even to attempt an answer, or had the authority to validate it, I would say above all that I do not believe there are inexorable dilemmas in history, since the latter is affected throughout as much by the powers of the spirit as it may be by those of the material order. I would say that, in addition to the factor of time, evolution has great weight in the resolution of situations that seem to be dilemmas, and that this evolution does not always favor the forces that are the most adapted to the given reality. I would say, finally, now with more specific reference to the case of Puerto Rico, that the present stage in which your nation is living is a sort of preparation for a subsequent synthesis. Once your economic development is consolidated, the habits of democratic life firmly rooted, your society organized with the desirable diversification of responsibilities and tasks, the techniques and measures of North American efficiency acquired, and once you have entered into the fulfillment of your own creative capacity in all realms, including that of culture, you will then be fully in a position to choose an historical channel in which your interests and your will may freely merge.

Until then—and I do not believe the time will be very distant—it is probable that the general circumstances of the world, and those of our America in particular, will prove advantageous for this synthesis. It is no show of divination to say that we are witnessing an historical mutation of incalculable importance. To think that the current tension to which all humanity finds itself subject—what we call the Cold War—could continue indefinitely, or even for a long time, is as unreasonable as it would be, on the other hand, to presume that this tension would be resolved exclusively in favor of one of the two poles or powers whose rivalry creates it. Neither will the forces of freedom succumb, nor will communism, once drained of its sectarian furies, prove useless to man as a demonstration of the efficacy that can be expected in the material domain by training individuals for collective responsibility. We still are not able to see the dialectical formula of the universal process of synthesis now getting under way, though it is already appearing on the world horizon and with it the necessity to safeguard it by both sides restraining their exclusivist pretentions. This universal synthesis will insist that the Western world put in motion all of its defensive powers and organize them conjointly. Our America will not escape this necessity. The dispersion and semirivalry in which we live will tend to be replaced by a coordination of powers, with each nation intelligently sacrificing unworthy particularisms, petty national jealousies, and desires prompted by excessive self-regard. Neither will the United States be able to continue demanding the unconditional acquiescence of these nations whose backing she needs as a basis for her own security, nor will our countries be able to continue squandering their energies in partisan and frontier squabbles in such disorderly fashion, missing the opportunities for concerted action and the urgencies of their common interests. Finally, we cannot allow the polemical commitments of Europe to intimidate our masses of ordinary people, diverting them from their democratic calling.

Indeed, we are approaching new forms of American understanding and cooperation in the years immediately ahead. What they will be and how they will come about I do not know. My adventure in prophecy does not go that far. But I do know that for these forms to be really effective they must be worthy, just, and balanced. Neither the intelligence nor the integrity of our peoples would lend themselves to anything else. And I believe it is very possible that the formula for this understanding is now being put together in Puerto Rico without our yet seeing it clearly. Far from being the submissive land of lackeyed obsequiousness that not a few superficial minds from outside imagine, this island is a field for experimentation in the new order of inter-American relations grounded in the freedom and dignity of all. It is so in the economic field. It will be so in the political field. It is becoming so in the cultural field, thanks to the fructifying effect of dialogue, of comparison of standards and methods and, I would say, even of souls.

Will Puerto Rico persist in the determination to be herself? Is she able, as it seems she will be, to continue defending her sensibility in the face of the incitements of a narrow type of utilitarianism? Will she give in to the temptation of an historical simplism that would change her from the cultural frontier of our Latin America into a sort of ghetto, a diaspora in an alien environment? Finally, precisely because she is so small geographically, will she apply herself, as Pedreira desired, to contemplating the depths and the heights? If she does all these things, then I think that to this generous people is reserved in the future the glory of having been able to offer itself as a sacrifice on the altar of America and of having emerged undamaged by its own generosity. All of us will then look upon it as the tenacious pioneer through whose effort the American frontier was brought into balance.

APPENDIX

Introduction

to the

University of Puerto Rico

Press Edition

Jorge Mañach

on His Last Frontier

H is love for Cuba, which made him prompt to sacrifice other attractive inclinations, was the essential axis on which the life and work of Jorge Mañach moved. It was the unchanging frontier from the beginning of his literary and political activities. These two occupations emerge in two early works: *The Crisis of High Culture in Cuba* (1925) and *Portraits of St. Christopher of Havana* (1926). They proceed to become broader and more profound in his great work as a journalist and in important later books: *Martí, Apostle of Freedom* (1933), *History and Style* (1944), *Examination of Quixotism* (1950), and *Toward a Philosophy of Life* (1951).

I pointed out these two concerns in the article "Jorge Mañach and Cuban Unrest" included in my book *Marks of Ibero-America* in 1936 and in my introduction of him at the theater of the University of Puerto Rico when he visited us in 1941 during a conference of writers. There I wished for him "the right balance between the two movements of your life for the good of American literature and the happiness of Cuba." This wish was gloriously fulfilled in his writings without the balance between the two concerns ever having been achieved in his personal life.

Mañach had a vocation for high culture, enriched by a period of extensive preparation at the universities of Havana, Harvard, Madrid, and Paris. But everywhere his love for Cuba, above all other loves, revealed itself in his nostalgia for her and his uneasiness on leaving her. His life was filled with painful preoccupation during the crises Cuba experienced. As he himself wrote: "These crises were times of indecision in facing a future involving quite different circumstances and realities." At such times he wanted to serve his country, overcoming his desire to return to his usual pursuits. Thus, he wrote to me in 1933: "With the fall of Machado* I wanted to leave

---

*Gerado Machado, tyrannical president of Cuba from 1925 to 1933.—Tr.

97

politics and return to my usual pursuits, to my work as a writer. It was not possible. The urgent feeling of responsibility in the situation obliged me to participate in the heated controversy. Then events descended on me, forcing me to accept the tremendous responsibility involved in heading the ministry of education. I tried to do all I was able in a troubled time, in which the revolutionary violence held in check for so many years was overflowing in a wild surge."

Mañach gave up his position; and Cuba, as he expressed it in the same letter, "slid down the slope into the military regime" that it shortly thereafter suffered under. This state of affairs, when he was on the verge of losing his life, obliged him to leave the country under diplomatic protection.

It was then that Federico de Onís repeated his invitation to teach at Columbia University. "Now I was able to accept without deserting," his valiant conscience said to me. He wanted to contribute to the *Revista Hispánica Moderna,* to intensify the attention paid to our culture. At his urging, a section on Hispanic-American studies was created at Columbia's Hispanic Institute and he was appointed its director.

He spent the summer of 1938 in the mountains of upstate New York and at the end of August he went to Cuba. There he found profound disquiet, but "immediate delight in her and in my friends and their affection." He was ready for another year of arduous work at Columbia, expecting it to be his last one there. His words then dispelled whatever shadow may have been visible on his highest love: "I want to return to Cuba. There is too much to be done there to continue deserting her in foreign academic latitudes. When I regain my country, you will regain our friendship in correspondence, because *then I shall once again be myself.*"

In 1959, after two and a half years in Europe, he wrote to me that he had returned to Cuba "with the breezes of freedom. . . . Here I am back at my old tasks: professorship, journalism, and no politics, although as to the latter, when you do not do it, they do it to you." He had finished the first volume of his *History of Philosophy* on which he had worked for fifteen years. After telling me of progress on this book, he added a revealing observation: "The world is shaking beneath our feet, and we all feel the need for a firmer spiritual grasp."

His last letter was in September 1960. The tragedy of his final political crisis can be conjectured from these words: "It will seem exaggerated to you," he wrote me, "but recently my life has scarcely had any rhythm or breaks *cum dignitate.*" At the end he informed me that it was practically certain he would come to Puerto Rico on the invitation of the rector and later president of our university, Jaime

Benítez. And he closed saying: "I cannot now tell you anything about the antecedents and the circumstances of this. Perhaps soon I can do so by word of mouth. I am only waiting for my passport. . . . I send you this news with a mixture of joy and melancholy."

He was already very ill and about to cross the dark frontier to exile. He came to us with the certainty of approaching death and a tremendous disappointment over the most painful political crisis of his life. But he proved himself brave to the last. Barely eight months of life remained for him and he devoted the major part of them to the preparation of the lectures that he was to give at the University of Puerto Rico, a project that was frustrated by death. The press of this institution now publishes them under the title of *Teoría de la frontera.*

A friend who lives in the house next to where Mañach spent these last months of his life told me that in the deep of night the tapping of his typewriter could be heard with urgent persistence in the silence. He wanted to outrun death and complete the brilliant exposition of his theory of the frontier.

The first three lectures were completed and left in good order, and appear here as chapters one, two, and three. With them were many pages grouped according to different aspects of the central theme, with crossed-out parts and handwritten notes, some very difficult to make out. I worked on these for long hours in order to bring coherence to the pages, which now constitute chapters four and five, ending with Mañach's dispassionate and affectionate study of the case of Puerto Rico.

As this posthumous work of Mañach thus appears, we have what many of us were waiting for: his thought concerning Hispanic America and the United States, inviting us to reflect, above all, on the case of Puerto Rico. *Teoría de la frontera* is the synthesis of the thought of Mañach, expressing his intelligence illumined by his love for America—our America—and his understanding of and fairness toward the other America. In his adventure in prophecy he is a generous contemplator of the political ideologies of all times, with a just outlook that is never deflected by blindness and personal disillusion.

In the beginning of the first lecture the broad contours of the theme are traced: "The frontier, particularly our cultural frontier with the United States, viewed not only on its own terms, but also insofar as it represents or symbolizes the actual and possible relations between the two Americas."

Mañach defines what the frontier is according to the geographers: "The limits or confines of a territory that is invested with a certain independence." Although terrestrial and maritime frontiers are designated, "the terrestrial ones are most characteristic since

only they confront . . . two zones of superior authority, two states."
Every frontier situation implies relations of physical contiguity and
of opposition, or at least of difference, between two complexes of
interests.

In this first lecture there are valuable clarifications about the
frontier and power, how frontiers originated and what their function
has been in history, concluding with the contrast that he points to
each time the two poles of his concern appear: the United States and
Hispanic America. Concerning the former, he accepts the thesis
of both Frederick Jackson Turner and George Santayana about the
national formation of the United States. "In the face of the expansive,
daring, pugnacious spirit of individual and autonomous effort that
the frontier created, Puritanism represented a certain counterweight
of moral discipline, destined in time to transcend its purely religious
bounds." Mañach later on depends on this thesis in his interpretation
of the relations between the United States and Hispanic America.

Mañach strongly delineates the influence of the frontier on our
America, too. What is peculiar about our situation is that its conquest
"produced as many frontiers as there were conquerors. Each one
first hatched its own colonial unity and later its respective independence and national character."

The battle with the Araucanos, about which Ercilla wrote, gave
Chile a strong national feeling. The Brazilian *bandeirantes* fed the first
impulses toward independence in that country. The imperialist dismemberment of Mexican territory by the United States still keeps
this sister nation feeling her northern frontier is "like the living flesh
of an amputated limb," inspiring an intense nationalism on that part
of the continent. The struggles and the shiftings of the frontier in
Argentina were not only a social and political stimulus, but also a
spiritual one, sublimated in literary form in the *Facundo* of Sarmiento,
the *Martín Fierro* of Hernández, and in the novel *Don Segundo Sombra*
by Güiraldes.

Political, ideological, and economic frontiers are taken up in the
second lecture. The style of life in both the democracies and the totalitarian regimes—fascist or communist—is described in this lecture,
the position of Mañach with respect to these frontiers thus definitely
becoming clear. For him, the greatest and most dramatic frontier
that divides the world today is the ideological one. The exposition of
this theme occupies more than a third of the lecture. He regrets that
the contemporary battle is formulated as a disjunction between
"capitalism" and "communism" because of the negative implications of the first term in the minds of most people and the positive
connotations of the second.

The commentary that follows is profound and illuminating, based on the lessons of history in which the author finds support to affirm his hope. The solution to the conflict between these ideologies cannot be violence, which would be not a solution but the dissolution of the entire civilized world and possible global destruction. Mañach does not see any possible conciliation, but he does believe in the possibility of a coexistence "that in the long run may turn out to be productive." He recognizes that the word coexistence today has hypocritical connotations. "But it is possible," he assures us, "that the reality itself, the balancing of the forces in conflict, will in the end make it an expression of sincerity."

In the third lecture he deals in general terms with the cultural frontier and arrives at this conclusion: "The cultural frontier is, strictly speaking, what separates and puts in opposition the masses who fall into our category called middle culture." These spiritual complexes are the ones that it is important to characterize in the investigation undertaken and the author uses the term "cultural frontier" in this sense in the comparison he makes of the two great American cultures that are the center of his interest.

In the midst of the richness of Mañach's thought and his consideration of problems of universal interest, beyond the pleasure with which his timely references captivate us, beyond the humor that at times comes out in his allusion to the abduction of Europe or the story of Lasserre about the efficacy of dialogue, let us, as Puerto Ricans, pause to reflect on those matters that concern us in these pages.

They concern us as an island, as a culture, as a country, and as an opportunity to contribute to the relations between the two great frontiers of our hemisphere. I know of nothing more profound and more replete with good will toward our land than the analysis Jorge Mañach has made—with all the generosity and seriousness that intelligence united with love were able to yield—of what he calls the case of Puerto Rico. Mañach contemplates us at a distance sufficient to be free of the passion that blinds. He is understanding in his loving observation, yet truthful and firm in what must be presented with veracity and firmness. And so he has set before our eyes our origins, our past, and our present and with a conciliatory generosity that is free of concessions begins his adventure into prophecy on which all of us must accompany him.

He starts with a question: "Do islands, because they are islands, have a distinct repertory of historical possibilities or a peculiar destiny?" As islanders this question interests us greatly. Mañach rejects the thesis of Angel Ganivet about the territorial spirit: What is characteristic of continental peoples is resistance; of peninsular peoples, independence; and of islanders, aggression. Mañach also rejects the idea that the islander has his defense in his isolation. We all know that our Antonio Pedreira considered insularity a limitation. Mañach does not believe in geographical determinism and at this point makes a statement that he will repeat in other passages of his study: "Geography alone does not make history; man creates history in a geographical setting."

The obstacles that a territory presents do no more than condition the human powers that are projected into it. What determines its destiny is the combination of the one with the other. Mañach thinks that this was the conviction of Pedreira in writing a book "apparently so negative but nevertheless deeply suffused with confidence in the will of his people," confidence that the Cuban essayist sees confirmed in later history.

Then he gives us his opinions. An island lacks frontiers in the strict geographical sense, since its immediate boundary is the sea. But the abundance of coasts and communications today make every island into a potential frontier. An island is "all pores." Influences come to it "as though filtered, and without as much impact as they have on terrestrial frontiers."

Size, and the fact that an island may be solitary or form part of an archipelago, also ought to be considered. If the archipelago has a single ruling power, it counts as a continent. This idea made Hostos think of the possibility of an Antilles confederation, which was frustrated by the forces of history.

Mañach also indicates how important for the destiny of an island is its being situated in the midst of great commercial routes or close to a center of political and economic power. If this center of power is very strong, the islands are attracted to its vortex. This last idea is illustrated by a simile, a graceful turn in prose nourished by classical roots and enlivened by modernity. The islands will be attracted to the vortex "as the floating leaves of a pool swirl around a fountain." In such cases, a tension between opinions equivalent to a frontier is produced in the insular environment. But none of this has a fatalistic tone to Mañach. That an island, or a constellation of islands, deals with these conditions successfully "depends on the intelligence and character of its people."

In the second lecture, "Political, Ideological, and Economic Frontiers," Mañach enters confidently into a discussion of the United States and ourselves, "ourselves" referring to Hispanic America, in which Puerto Rico stands out as an intensely interesting component. The speaker declares that his intent is not to excuse anyone for anything. He will speak of our great neighbor "with objectivity, . . . sincerity, and when appropriate, with severity or with praise." He thinks that estimations of the United States, particularly in the past fifty years, have been shot through—the word is particularly expressive—and still are, of stereotypic judgments and crude simplifications.

In this tranquil position, he begins by noting that Spain's declining power after the seventeenth century coincided with the rise in North America of a "deliberate and vigorous" will to empire. This will extended itself by advancing its frontiers. The characteristics that carried out this task were a fighting spirit, aggressiveness, a taste for risk and adventure, confidence in one's own powers, and the exercise of personal will—characteristics that later decided the independence of the colonies. Then the states united and conceived the idea of rounding out their territory. The weakness of Spain facilitated the first stage of the effort. Jefferson spoke of "manifest destiny" in an expansive vision that perhaps extended to the isthmus connecting the two Americas.

Monroe traced—theoretically—the most vast frontier known: The European powers must not impede the will of a United States now "powerful and great." The advance of control left its trail in Mexico and Central America. All of this culminated in Senator Hawley's question at a banquet: "When we rule over the continent without rivals, what kind of civilization will we have?" The voice of Martí, who was then in the United States preparing for the independence of Cuba and Puerto Rico, answered him: "A dreadful one, in truth: that of Carthage!"

The result of that expansion was independence, with the Platt Amendment for Cuba and a change of masters for the Philippines and Puerto Rico. But since the master was a stranger to the language, the tradition, and the customs, the political and cultural destiny of Puerto Rico was compromised.

Mañach asks himself at this point: Why did this expansion stop in the Antilles? He sees the episodes that occurred later in Panama, the Dominican Republic, and Guatemala as having different motivations from that of pure expansive ambition. The subsequent conduct of the United States makes it credible that she did not act with a true imperialistic purpose. He concludes: The Philippines are free; the Platt Amendment was withdrawn from Cuba; Puerto Rico is a "free associated state" and will have her independence when she desires it. Mañach is not unaware of the realistic calculations that may have influenced this restraint by the United States. But again he asks himself: Would other powerful nations have been satisfied with this?

He also sees a realistic-idealistic polarity in the United States that makes her appear to err in her foreign relations. He comments in detail on this aspect in relation to often reprehensible Hispanic-American political situations. Following her economic interests and the international political order, the United States has compromised with the excessive authoritarianism in those countries. In the face of oppressive governments, the principle of nonintervention has not been fulfilled at the insistence of the democratic elements who were themselves injured by the oppressive regimes—a conflict between norm and reality.

I leave without a summary the contrast of cultures: one of action, the other of sensibility. In the pages arranged under the heading "The Contemporary Situation on the Frontier" appears the essential role that Mañach assigns to dialogue. The résumé of the French novelette by Pierre Lasserre, *The Unusual Stroll,* serves Mañach as a planned introduction to the theme of America and Puerto Rico.

In the contemplation of our hemisphere, Mañach sees himself divided between the freethinker and the priest of *The Unusual Stroll;* between Anglo-Saxon rationality and Latin sensibility. He knew that we Puerto Ricans do not like to be compared to a bridge between two cultures, for a "bridge is something over which people walk, and you rightly would not want to bear the impress of wayfarers' feet." He proposes that we call the whole Caribbean area the town square of the hemisphere. If the Mexican frontier is a trench where "fears and suspicions are increasingly being dissipated, the Antilles are benches that invite relaxation and dialogue." And too, in Mañach's view, it has been Puerto Rico's lot to be the most accessible in this meeting of cultures "not because of geography but by accident of history."

We can make of *The Unusual Stroll,* and the lesson derived from it, an introduction to the last and most significant theme for us in this grappling of Mañach with all the frontiers.

Our good friend asks our permission to discuss, "with all possible delicacy," what he calls a theme that touches us to the quick. The case of Puerto Rico is the very model of the frontier theme, and Mañach thinks that not to go into it would be unforgivable. He states that he will not allow himself to intrude into the question of what constitutional status Puerto Rico should have, for this "is a matter that is entirely up to you to decide." What is indispensable is to look at the problem without reservations and with all the facts.

He first considers two aspects: the exact relation in which Puerto Rico stands with respect to the rest of America, and what problems and prospects are created for her by the peculiarity of this situation. Mañach concludes that Puerto Rico is a piece of Hispanic America from the spiritual standpoint. He describes the political link with the United States as an abrupt occurrence that from the beginning was not invested with any juridical formality, but was a bare fact of military occupation. The subsequent modifications in this situation are important but do not "alter the linkage itself in its essence."

He defines the case of Puerto Rico thus: both her "soul and body are outside the borders of the United States; but at the same time she finds herself in an historical situation that tends to sever these two parts of her being—to unite her in spirit with the nation to the north, while her body remains among us as a mere geographical testimony to her Hispanic-American past."

Under these circumstances is Puerto Rico a frontier? Mañach asks himself. Is it one of Latin America with the United States or of the United States with Latin America? (Mañach uses "Latin" or "Hispanic" interchangeably to designate our America.) In his questions he sees several Latin American attitudes toward Puerto Rico. Some see our island voluntarily surrendered to the United States. Others pity her as "Little Red Riding Hood" gone astray in the wolf's territory who must be rescued from the consequences of her own innocence.

Then he tells us the bitter truth that, in our internal affairs, all of us keep alive through our effort to be ourselves. He does so in the form of a question that gives his words dramatic intensity: "How can we deny that the conflict between the Hispanic tradition and the political link generates, among yourselves, a whole group of tensions and equivocations, of hesitations with respect to the present and the future, which disturb the Puerto Rican soul with concern about its proper destiny?"

He declares that, as he sees it, Puerto Rico is a frontier on account of something more than her geographical position, namely, on account of "forces of opposition and resistance that are *still* rooted in her history and her culture." This persistent reality makes her *yet* a frontier of Latin America itself toward the north and not the inverse. She is not a political frontier, but she is indeed "a cultural frontier *sui generis.*"

The great problem of Puerto Rico, according to Mañach, revolves around the way in which the time adverbs *still* and *yet* are to be resolved. If the conditions to which they point are consolidated so that their transitoriness disappears, the problem reduces itself to a question. To what point would the cultural frontier be able to stand up against the nonexistence of a political frontier and an economic frontier?

For lack of space, I omit the profound reflections that this question arouses in Mañach. I pass on at once to his résumé of our history and its consequences from the colonial era until today. Two epochs unfold before his view: one of discouragement and defeatism, the other of overcoming.

During the first he describes us as feeling ourselves caught in an inexorable destiny. The visit of José Vasconcelos—this seems to me an interpretation with deep meaning—when he exhorted the youth of Puerto Rico to independence at any cost, seems to Mañach an unconscious cruelty: "Treating as feasible, though with heroism, something that at the time there were reasons to consider impossible."

Mañach thinks that this urging, coupled with the example of Ireland, had much to do with the budding of certain plans for resolving the problem of Puerto Rico by violence. And he adds: "The very disparity between the recommended cure and the experienced reality helped to accentuate the feeling of frustration that it aimed to remove."

This feeling of frustration was what brought to the poetry of José de Diego not a "sweet nostalgia for unrealized ideals," as Mañach writes, but a despair, as evident in the upsetting conclusions of such poems as "Alleluias," "Night Soul," and "The Last String." In Lloréns Torres's work, it is not just a matter of idealization; the frustration also brought him to desperate rejection in the sonnet "Puerto Rico": "The Yankee was never ours, nor will he ever be!" Mañach's comment on the verse of Palés Matos, "Puerto Rico, good-for-nothing," is more correct.

Mañach's reflections on destiny lead him to see it as a cross or adjustment between what man desires and what is possible. Quoting Ortega y Gasset, whom he knows thoroughly and whom he accompanies in the highest flights of thought, Mañach describes this cross as one "between man and his circumstances." We cannot choose the circumstances, but we can choose our attitude in the face of them.

The second significant period in our history, according to Mañach, is what he calls "the overcoming." This time he begins with a series of questions. I shall quote only the first one, which summarizes them all: "What mysterious forces—mysterious sometimes because of their unexpected existence, at other times because of the imponderable and unforeseeable character of their operation—are the ones then that come to the rescue of the destiny of nations?"

The work of awakening and renewal was done by Muñoz Marín and those who worked with him. Mañach thinks that the "persuasive patience" of Muñoz Marín has brought about a veritable revolution in Puerto Rico "in the most positive and substantial sense of that well-worn word."

"When it seemed that your people were already in danger of seduction by alien styles of life, your poets and prose writers came forth saying . . . that doing and having are enterprises in which men can imitate one another with impunity, but that one cannot renounce what is his own without being a counterfeiter. . . . I believe that today it can be said, not that Puerto Rico has a soul, but that she has recovered it."

Before beginning what he calls an "Adventure in Prophecy," he repeats: "Puerto Rico has found her soul. It is still a soul unsure of its destiny, but it is a soul concerned about it."

In his adventure in prophecy another question awaits us: "Do these tensions of which I have just spoken represent true dilemmas, or on the contrary, are they generated between goals that are capable of reconciliation?" Mañach does not believe that there are inexorable destinies in history, because the latter are affected throughout as much by the powers of the spirit as they may be by those of the material order. Time and evolution inevitably leave their mark. The present for Puerto Rico is a time of preparation for a synthesis in which "Once your economic development is consolidated, the habits of democratic life firmly rooted, your society organized with the desirable diversification of responsibilities and tasks, the techniques and measures of North American efficiency acquired, and you have entered into the fulfillment of your own creative capacity in all realms, including that of culture, you will then be fully in a position to choose an historical channel in which your interests and your will may freely merge."

He believes that it is probable that before long the general conditions of the world, and of our America in particular, will prove favorable to this synthesis. New forms of understanding and of cooperation are already in view for the years ahead.

Our thinker concludes with a declaration about what he knows and what he expects. He knows that the effective forms must be worthy, just, and balanced. He believes it is very possible that the formula for this understanding is being put together in Puerto Rico without our seeing it yet.

Far from being submissive and subject, as superficial minds outside imagine, this island "is a field for experimentation in the new order of inter-American relations grounded in the freedom and dignity of all. It is so in the economic field. It will be so in the political field. It is becoming so in the cultural field, thanks to the fructifying effect of dialogue, of comparison of standards and methods, and I would say, even of souls."

One of the articles in *The Living Past,* a book in which Jorge Mañach collected part of his newspaper writings, bears the title "The Crisis of Hope." This crisis was repeated in his life during his political career. He came out of it, as he confesses in one of his letters, by allegorically living through José Enrique Rodó's parable "The Flower in the Vase."

The parable concerns a child who was playing in a garden, rhythmically striking a glass vase with a stick. Then the child changed his game and filled the vase with sand. Trying again to bring out the ring of the glass, he discovered it had fallen silent. Checking a tear, he looked around, saw a white flower, appropriated it with an assist from the wind, fixed the stem in the same sand that had made the soul of the vase fall silent, and lifted the flower aloft and paraded it in triumph through the garden.

After one of his crises of hope in Cuba—the failure of his projects in the ministry of education—he wrote to me from Columbia University: "I put my enthusiasm into the teaching of the literature of our America as director of Hispanic-American studies at the Hispanic Institute. I am realizing in myself that parable of Rodó: that of the flower in the vase."

It was also a crisis of hope, the most painful of all, the last in his life, that obliged him to cross the frontier of exile. In another university, that of Puerto Rico, he prepared and fixed the stem of a new flower: the lectures that constitute this book. He will not be able, like the child in the parable, to dry a tear and, smiling, lift high the new flower born on his last frontier. But the publication of this book now lifts it, and it will continue to be lifted by those who read its pages with understanding.

CONCHA MELENDEZ

Santurce, Puerto Rico
September 1969